AFFIRMATIVE ACTION AND BLACK ENTREPRENEURSHIP

AFFIRMATIVE ACTION AND BLACK ENTREPRENEURSHIP

Thomas D. Boston

A Century Foundation Book

London and New York

First published 1999
by Routledge
11 New Fetter Lane, London EC4P 4EE

Simultaneously published in the USA and Canada
by Routledge
29 West 35th Street, New York, NY 10001

© 1999 The Century Foundation

Typeset in Garamond by Routledge
Printed and bound in Great Britain by
Clays Ltd, St. Ives PLC

British Library Cataloging in Publication Data
A catalogue record for this book is available from the British Library

Library of Congress Cataloging in Publication Data
A catalogue record for this book has been requested

ISBN 0–415–09594–8

TO MY SON LINJE AND DAUGHTER
SHANI

CONTENTS

TABLES

FOREWORD

For centuries, immigrants came to America seeking religious toler-
ance, political freedom, and, perhaps most of all, economic
opportunity. That generalization, of course, loses all its force in the
exceptional case of African-Americans. Not only were Africans
forcibly transplanted from their homes, they were delivered to
America in order to serve the economic interests of slaveholders.
After the Civil War, despite the rhetoric of "forty acres and a mule,"
virtually all of the newly freed slaves found themselves without
economic resources. Moreover, the relatively rapid establishment of
tenant-farming arrangements that, in many ways, were similar to
serfdom stunted opportunities for economic progress for generations
of Southern blacks. Not surprisingly, then, a significant part of
black history since emancipation can be understood as an effort to
catch up and share in American opportunity and prosperity.

There was some progress in the 1930s and 1940s in terms of
industrial employment. During that same period, small, black-
owned businesses flourished in black communities. But it was not
until the decades following 1960 that there was enough steady
advancement to allow blacks to think realistically about achieving
the American dream – a dream that traditionally implied ownership
of a home and even a business.

The gains in employment, the professions, and education were an
important stage in the long journey toward economic equality, but
it is a journey that is far from over. Incomes of blacks and whites
remain significantly different, and data on wealth show an even
more dramatic disparity. The latter measure is a reflection of several
factors, including the obviously greater difficulty of saving if one
has a modest income. It also is related to the still limited equity and
business ownership by African-Americans.

Despite international mega-mergers, small businesses remain not only numerous – of the 23.3 million nonfarm businesses in the US, 99 percent employ fewer than five hundred people – but also the nation's principal engine of job creation. In politics there is no controversy about the desirability of small business creation and little doubt that government should try to help small businesses to succeed. This consensus, however, breaks down when it comes to certain critical issues affecting minority-owned businesses.

A generation ago, governments at all levels enacted laws and began programs designed to increase black ownership of businesses. So-called minority set-asides in contracts, as well as other devices, were an attempt to level the playing field, offering black-owned businesses a way to overcome the "old boy networks" that kept them from many opportunities such as subcontracting in the construction business. The range of programs also involved assistance regarding access to capital, training, and technical advice. These programs, combined with independent successes by minority entrepreneurs, became symbols of the first significant movement of black Americans into the company of proprietors and managers. In some communities – Atlanta is a notable example – these firms became a real engine of local prosperity.

Despite or perhaps because of these successes, the current assault upon affirmative action of all types seems to be politically irresistible. Anti-affirmative-action legislative initiatives and state referenda abound. A series of Supreme Court decisions also have sharply constrained the legal basis for such programs. While there has been substantial news coverage of these developments, there is good reason to believe that most Americans have only the fuzziest notions about how affirmative action works in practice. The need for clear reporting and analysis on this issue has never been greater,

In the pages that follow Thomas Boston, professor of economics at Georgia Institute of Technology and former senior economist to the Joint Economic Committee of Congress, helps to fill that need, tracing the development of programs that have encouraged minority ownership and success in business. Using Atlanta as a case study, he shows how affirmative action programs in procurement worked in practice. He examines the backlash against these programs represented by a series of court challenges, culminating in the *Richmond* v. *Croson* decision by the U.S. Supreme Court. Those decisions have made it difficult, if not impossible, to continue the sort of active government encouragement of minority-owned businesses that brought about the successes in Atlanta. Boston chronicles the growth of black firms and analyzes how the legal environment is likely to affect them in the future. He goes further, proposing specific policies designed to make possible a renewal of activist government in this area. After reporting on the current status of black Americans and the impact of today's national prosperity on them, he argues that growth alone will not close the gap in wealth and income between whites and blacks.

Affirmative Action and Black Entrepreneurship continues a long tradition of Century Foundation/Twentieth Century Fund books examining inequality and social programs designed to alleviate it, from Robert Haveman's *Starting Even*, to John Sibley Butler and Charles Moskos's exploration of the army's efforts to ensure equality in *All That We Can Be*, to James K. Galbraith's exploration of the issue of economic inequality in *Created Unequal: The Crisis in American Pay* and Edward N. Wolff's look at the subject in *Top Heavy: A Study of the Increasing Inequality of Wealth in America*.

On behalf of the Trustees of The Century Foundation, I thank Professor Boston for this important contribution to our understanding of the nature of black entrepreneurship, its contribution to raising the socioeconomic status of African-Americans, and the appropriate role for public policy in fostering minority business success.

Richard C. Leone, President
The Century Foundation
June 1998

ACKNOWLEDGMENTS

Beverly Goldberg of The Century Foundation encouraged me to undertake this research. I am deeply indebted to her and to the Foundation for generous support and enduring patience. I also thank Dave Smith and Kathleen Quinn of the Foundation for helping me focus the arguments of the book.

Tim Bates provided a great deal of encouragement and many insightful comments on this book. But, more importantly, he planted the seeds of so many ideas that are explored in detail here. Thanks Tim and thanks also to Andrew F. Brimmer and Margaret C. Simms for helpful comments on chapters of the book that were presented at professional meetings. Without the cooperation and assistance of Sue Ross and Michael Sullivan, former Directors of the Office of Contract Compliance at the City of Atlanta, and Michael Cooper, Director of the Office of Contract Compliance at Fulton County, Georgia, this research would not have been possible. I also thank former Mayors Maynard Jackson and Andrew Young, and current Mayor Bill Campbell for letting me assist in the planning, development and implementation of Atlanta's Equal Business Opportunity Program. I thank the directors of the following organizations for endorsing this research and cooperating with me in its conduct: the Atlanta Business League, Georgia Minority Supplier Development Council, Office of Contract Compliance at the Atlanta Public School System, Office of Contract Compliance of the Metropolitan Atlanta Rapid Transit System, Office of Contract Compliance of Dekalb County, and Grady Health Systems Office of Disadvantaged Business Enterprises. Finally, I thank Wanda Gail Greene, Krista Tillery and Tarek Saoud for their research assistance.

INTRODUCTION

The number of black-owned businesses is increasing at twice the rate of all small businesses in the United States. Between 1982 and 1992, the latest period for which census of minority business data are available, black-owned businesses increased by 7.3 percent annually and their employment capacity grew by 11 percent annually. Even though they account for just 3.6 percent of all small firms and 1 percent of small business revenue, their growth trend is impressive. Assuming the current growth rate can be sustained through the first decade of the next century, black-owned businesses will number well over 2 million.

Today, these businesses have an employment capacity that is equivalent to about 3 percent of the black workforce, but if they can sustain their current growth rate, by the year 2010 they will have an employment capacity large enough to accommodate 12 to 17 percent of the 2010 black workforce. Of course, this assumes that future conditions will be similar to present conditions. But present conditions are changing rapidly and one significant development that will likely slow the growth of black-owned businesses is the demise of affirmative action programs for minority-owned businesses.

This book examines the growth and changing profile of black-owned businesses. In the process, it demonstrates the importance of minority procurement programs in creating opportunities for market entry, diversification and growth. By allowing black entrepreneurs to break out of personal service and retail activities and to enter dynamically growing industries, these programs helped catalyze the growth of a second generation of black-owned businesses. Atlanta is used as a case study, but this book's lessons are applicable nationwide.

In 1975 Atlanta established the country's first minority business affirmative action plan at the local level. Its significance resided in the fact that it was not tied to a federal mandate and its goals greatly exceeded those proposed at the federal level. Over a quarter of a century later, the Atlanta metropolitan area has the nation's fastest growing black business sector and it has one of the country's most successful cadres of black business owners.

This book has a compelling story to tell. It will show how and why black-owned businesses were able to break out of their traditional concentration in personal service and retail activities, the so-called "mom and pop" enterprises, and diversify into dynamically growing industries. Affirmative action programs provided the catalyst for this diversification.

As racial barriers crumbled and society opened new opportunities, a second generation of black-owned businesses emerged. Many of the owners of these enterprises were graduates of the nation's leading business schools and had acquired managerial experience in some of the country's largest corporations. The new business opportunities made available through public sector procurement programs converged with the enhanced education and business experience of blacks, and the outcome changed the character of black-owned businesses. Not only did these new businesses operate in non-traditional industries, they were less dependent on black consumers. In fact, a significant portion of their revenue is generated in the public sector. Their owners are usually young, well educated and much more experienced in business activities than the black entrepreneurs that preceded them.

The truly successful companies of this second generation are typically non-public multi-million-dollar corporations whose ownership is closely held by the founders, family members and sometimes a few company executives. Their growth strategies center on securing debt as a source of growth and expansion, rather than considering a merger, acquisition or sharing equity in the company. A classic example of the impact of affirmative action is the H.J. Russell & Company of Atlanta. Starting out as a relatively small-scale construction company in 1952, its participation on large public works projects over the years allowed it to become a diversified, multi-million-dollar corporation. Today it operates in construction contracting, property management, airport concessions and real estate development. In 1996, the company's workforce was over 1,400 and its annual revenue was $163 million. The company has been ranked consistently among *Black Enterprise Magazine*'s 100 largest industrial and service companies. Without question the H.J. Russell Company could not have achieved this growth without skilled leadership. But the watershed for its phenomenal growth can be traced to the opportunities made available by the affirmative action program in Atlanta. Indeed, the compelling message of this book is that *opportunity matters*! So Atlanta's story is a simple one: create opportunities and black businesses will follow.

The city is often referred to as the "Black Mecca," but there is nothing supernatural happening in Atlanta. True, it is growing rapidly in population and income, but several metropolitan areas across the country are experiencing similar growth trends. What distinguishes Atlanta from other places is the real and perceived opportunities created by the minority business affirmative action programs at numerous agencies in the city and metropolitan area. Whenever opportunities and normal rewards for risk-taking exist, entrepreneurs will respond whether they are black, white, red or brown. Atlanta's experience proves that entrepreneurship is not dependent upon the culture of a people, and developing black-owned businesses can be accelerated if racial barriers are reduced.

At a time when black-owned businesses are growing faster than ever before, affirmative action programs are under attack. In 1989 and then again in 1995, the U.S. Supreme Court rendered decisions that have led to the dismantling of dozens of minority procurement programs. The late Supreme Court Justice Thurgood Marshall predicted that the "strict scrutiny" standard, which requires an exacting proof of discrimination as a precondition for an affirmative action program, would have a "daunting" impact. When the Court implemented this standard, Marshall argued that it closed its eyes to "constitutional history and social reality."[1]

This book traces the impact of Supreme Court guidelines on minority business affirmative action programs and on the development of black-owned businesses. The Supreme Court decisions have forced local and state agencies to spend millions upon millions of dollars in futile attempts to meet the new standard. One by one these agencies have failed, not because discrimination does not exist but because the burden of proof is prohibitively expensive and the method for establishing it is not clearly spelled out by the Supreme Court. Strict scrutiny, Marshall correctly observed, is "strict in theory and fatal in fact."

Among other things, this book recommends that a Judicial Commission be established to clarify the guidelines of strict scrutiny. In the absence of this step, the Court's pronouncement that race-based remedies for prior discrimination are constitutional is true only in principle. The current gap between theory and reality on this issue is vast and reminds one of the time early in this country's history when it proclaimed that "all men are created equal," but counted blacks as three fifths of a person.

If the current anti-affirmative action trend continues and the courts do not spell out more clearly the guidelines for achieving strict scrutiny, society will renege on its obligation to remedy historical injustices. Additionally, it will lose an opportunity to assist in the promotion of a business strategy that has the potential to reduce black income and employment disparities enormously.

While the economic growth and population growth of a local area are important ingredients in black-business growth, these businesses must have the opportunity to enter diverse industries in the public and private sectors to sustain broad-based revenue and employment gains. Historically, racial discrimination excluded black businesses from public sector contracting and procurement, but the rise of affirmative action programs across the country in the early 1980s reversed this. By the end of the 1980s almost 200 programs existed at the state and local levels. Many cities patterned their programs after the City of Atlanta's plan. In fact, Atlanta's program has sometimes been referred to as "the granddaddy of set-aside programs."

In 1975, Maynard Jackson, the city's first black mayor, established a requirement that 25 percent of the $1 billion in planned construction expenditures on the new international airport terminal be made with minority contractors. Jackson's policy was a response to the fact that in 1973, the year he was elected, black contractors were awarded only $41,800 of the total contracting expenditures made by the city. In fact, this was the first year that city records show any procurement award being made to black-owned businesses. The steps taken by Jackson to remedy one hundred years of discriminatory practices were emulated across the country on a less grand scale.

Since their inception, minority business programs have been the focus of legal challenges. However, the 1980 U.S. Supreme Court decision in the case of *Fullilove* v. *Klutznick*[2] was broadly interpreted by state and local areas as giving constitutional legitimacy to these affirmative action efforts. In reality, the decision only addressed the constitutionality of the federal set-asides. Nevertheless, following the Fullilove Decision, affirmative action programs were established across the country and continued to grow until the 1989 Croson Decision.

On 23 January 1989, a majority of Justices on the U.S. Supreme

Court ruled for the first time that "strict scrutiny" would be applied to determine the constitutionality of all state and local minority business programs involving racial mandates. In lay terms, this means that a governmental agency must demonstrate, through elaborate research known as a disparity study, that its contracting operations have directly or indirectly discriminated against a minority group before it can establish a race-based remedy. While the notion of establishing a record of past discrimination rather than relying on broad societal trends seems reasonable, the strict scrutiny standard has the potential to make this requirement very exacting.

Within two years of the Croson Decision, thirty-three of the nation's minority business programs were disbanded, sixty-six faced legal challenges and sixty-five were substantially revised. By 1991, local governments were spending an average of a quarter of a million dollars in consultant fees on disparity studies to meet the Croson standard of strict scrutiny. The cost of these studies was driven to such prohibitive levels because the Supreme Court gave very broad guidelines in the Croson Decision on how this standard should be met.

So, local governments commissioned consultants to conduct the research needed to meet the Croson standard. But consultants were unsure just what evidence and what methodology were appropriate for complying with the strict scrutiny. The lack of more precise directions from the Court increased the cost of disparity studies by forcing consultants to examine many types of extraneous evidence. During subsequent court proceedings, much of this evidence often turned out to be irrelevant.

These broad guidelines of the Croson Decision are haunting almost every local area that has commissioned a disparity study. No matter how much they spend, affirmative action programs and the studies upon which they are based are sued and discredited in one legal battle after another. The opponents of affirmative action have exploited the ambiguities of the strict scrutiny standard to undermine the credibility of disparity studies. They do this by attempting to define "the" research standard for conducting the studies and by trying to persuade courts to accept their views. Not surprisingly, this so-called "standard" has changed over time and it is vague and impractical on many methodological issues. In addition, it is enormously costly to comply with.

The irony is that affirmative action programs will still be challenged in court no matter how much money is spent. When studies do not comply with the so-called "standard" that is promoted by the opponents of affirmative action, they are labeled "fatally flawed." Thurgood Marshall was wise enough to recognize the problems inherent in applying the strict scrutiny standard to minority procurement programs.

Professor George La Noue, a consultant whose services are frequently engaged by opponents of affirmative action programs, has authored an influential article that he has entitled a "standard" for conducting disparity studies.[3] In recent expert testimony, La Noue indicates that he has reviewed thirty to forty disparity studies. When asked if any would satisfy the standard, as he interprets it, La Noue replied, "No."[4]

This raises the broader issue of fairness. For example, suppose the situation were reversed and an influential proponent of affirmative action defined the "standard" of evidence that must be met before an affirmative action program can be established. Furthermore, suppose the standard was based on determining whether a disparity exists between the share of an agency's awards that go to minorities and the share of minorities in the population. This would not sit well with opponents of affirmative action because the standard does not take into consideration the share of businesses that are willing, qualified and capable of engaging in government contracting. Instead it is simply derived from a population proportion. But who cares about their objections, because in my hypothetical example the opponents are not the ones who define matters? In such a hypothetical situation, a non-minority contractor would be disadvantaged from the very beginning in exercising his or her constitutional rights to equal treatment because the standard of evidence for the preference is biased in favor of those who wish to have affirmative action programs. Blacks find themselves in an analogous situation today. Specifically, one of the most important aspects of the strict scrutiny standard of evidence is the definition of a willing, able and qualified firm. But currently, opponents of affirmative action have influenced this definition heavily and, as one might imagine, it is defined in such a way as to bias research against finding a racial disparity in government contracting.

For blacks and other historically disadvantaged minorities to enjoy the constitutional guarantees of equal protection and due process, the requirements of strict scrutiny must be clarified and established objectively. The U.S. Supreme Court had an opportunity to do this in both the Croson Decision and the Adarand Decision.[5] But those decisions were vague on methodology. This is why it is important to establish a Judicial Commission on Strict Scrutiny standards for race-based minority procurement programs. The Commission should develop the specific evidentiary guidelines and enumerate the appropriate research methodology for strict scrutiny.

In a speech to the nation on affirmative action, President Bill Clinton defended his belief in the concept and pointed to Atlanta as an example of the racial progress that such policies can bring about. Affirmative action has created significant advances in that city, especially within the black business sector. Atlanta illustrates the simple fact that *opportunity matters*.

The arguments of this book draw heavily upon the author's detailed study of black-owned businesses in the Atlanta metropolitan area. As an economic advisor to the city's current Mayor, Bill Campbell, and advisor to past Mayor, Maynard Jackson, the author has been closely involved with the city's minority business program and has aided in the establishment of its goals. These experiences have demonstrated that black-owned businesses can flourish in environments having the right combination of economic growth and equal opportunity.

One way to "mend" rather than "end" affirmative action, is to make sure that fair, objective and reasonable standards exist for determining the legitimacy of claims of racial discrimination. When this is done, strict scrutiny will no longer be strict in theory and fatal in fact.

In the first chapter of this book, the evolution of affirmative action programs in procurement at the federal and local levels is discussed. Using Atlanta as a case study, this chapter reveals how that city was the first to implement an affirmative action program and how cities across the country followed its lead. The operation of these programs was a watershed in the development of black-owned businesses and facilitated their diversification from a concentration in personal service and retail industries to more dynamically growing industries. The chapter's central message is that opportunity matters.

Chapter 2 examines the circumstances leading to the passage of the U.S. Supreme Court decision in the case of *City of Richmond* v. *J.A. Croson Company*. Strict scrutiny has become the new legal standard for race preference programs seeking to remedy the effects of past discriminatory practices. The problem is, the guidelines for meeting this new standard are vague, and as a result local governments have spent millions of dollars in vain attempts to comply. The late Supreme Court Justice Thurgood Marshall called strict scrutiny, "strict in theory and fatal in fact." The impact of this new standard on black-owned businesses is examined.

Chapter 3 examines the characteristics of the new generation of black-owned businesses that have emerged in Atlanta over the last two decades. It looks at who these businesses employ, where their employees reside, where the businesses are located, and the educational and management background of their owners. Blacks and other hard-pressed inner city residents still shoulder a disproportionate share of unemployment. But this chapter shows how Atlanta's promotion of black-owned businesses is helping to generate jobs and narrow the racial unemployment gap.

During the period of racial segregation, the historic environment in Atlanta and other cities was characterized by discriminatory actions that increased the risk of operating in industries outside of the narrowly proscribed fields of personal service and retail activities. But despite these racial barriers, a viable black business sector did evolve, and today this sector is much more diversified and provides jobs for almost 6 percent of the city's workforce. Chapter 4 sketches the historical environment as a backdrop for explaining the current state of black-owned businesses.

Chapter 5 focuses on the factors that are responsible for the current lag in black entrepreneurship. It examines the typical path to an entrepreneurship career and the characteristics and attributes associated with business ownership. The chapter shows how entrepreneurs respond to rewards and risk, and how the absence of normal expected returns adversely affected the evolution of black-owned businesses.

Chapter 6 calls for the establishment of a Judicial Commission on Strict Scrutiny. Because the Croson Decision outlines broad categories of evidence, consultants and lower courts have provided their own interpretation of the meaning of strict scrutiny. This has led to tremendous variance in the kinds of data and information examined, and the specific approaches employed. It has also made disparity studies extremely expensive and minority business affirmative action programs easy targets for legal suits. Most local programs are experiencing legal challenges or threats of legal challenges. Yet the method for complying with the strict scrutiny standard is still vague. In addition, opponents of affirmative action are influencing it. As long as this is the case, the constitutional guarantees under the Fourteenth Amendment will be difficult for minorities to realize. For this reason, Chapter 6 concludes that a

Judicial Commission on Strict Scrutiny standards must be established.

Chapter 7 discusses "Twenty by Ten," a strategy for black business and employment growth in the twenty-first century. In plain language, it means that the government and private sector should pursue policies that are designed to create a sufficient number of black-owned firms such that their combined employment capacity will be equal to 20 percent of the black labor force by the year 2010. The chapter examines the current status of black Americans and the impact of the current expansion on their economic fortunes. The conclusion is that economic growth is necessary to close the gap between blacks and whites, but growth alone is not sufficient. It argues for policies aimed at targeting the growth of black-owned businesses because of the contribution these businesses make to black employment. The chapter closes with a discussion of strategies the country should consider to maintain its commitment to the growth of minority-owned businesses.

1

OPPORTUNITY MATTERS

The evolution of affirmative action programs

During the 1950s, the U.S. Supreme Court rendered several important decisions that struck at the foundation of Jim Crow segregation. In 1954 the Court ruled in the case of *Brown* v. *Board of Education, Topeka, Kansas* that racial segregation in elementary public education is unconstitutional. In 1955 and 1956, it ruled in the cases of *Mayor of Baltimore* v. *Dawson* and of *Gayle* v. *Browder* that racial discrimination in access to public beaches and public buses is unconstitutional. Then, in 1958, the Court outlawed discrimination in access to public parks in the case of *New Orleans City Park Association* v. *Detiege*. Finally, in 1963, the Court even had to ban discrimination in access to state courtrooms in the case of *Johnson* v. *Virginia*.

These legal victories fueled social protest movements during the 1960s and civil rights demonstrations, sit-ins and freedom rides, and boycotts swept the South. By the mid-1960s urban rebellions engulfed the inner cities of the North. Faced with this growing racial discontent, President Lyndon Johnson persuaded Congress to address the nation's 300-year-old legacy of racial discrimination.

Congress passed the 1964 Civil Rights Act authorizing the Attorney General to enforce the Fourteenth Amendment to the Constitution. This amendment had been adopted in 1868 to prevent states from denying equal protection to freed slaves. Titles II and III of the 1964 Act forbade discrimination in public accommodation. Title IV authorized the Attorney General to implement the 1954 U.S. Supreme Court decision in the case of *Brown* v. *Board of Education* that outlawed segregated public educational facilities.

In 1965, the federal government attacked employment discrimination with Executive Order 11246.[1] This Order and its amendment obligated recipients of federal contracts in excess of $50,000 to file written affirmative action plans, not to discriminate in employment, and to undertake affirmative steps to recruit and upgrade minorities and women. The Labor Department was empowered to enforce the Order and to impose penalties for non-compliance.

The momentum surrounding equal rights eventually spilled over into the minority business arena. The Economic Opportunity Act of 1964 directed the Small Business Administration (SBA) to assist small businesses owned by low-income individuals. In 1967, the federal government amended this Act and provided the first statutory assistance to minority-owned small businesses.

During the Presidential Campaign of 1968, candidate Richard Nixon promoted the philosophy of "black capitalism." It was thought that the creation of a viable black business class would help diffuse the urban rebellions engulfing American cities. In March of 1969, Nixon issued Executive Order 11458, which outlined arrangements for developing and coordinating a national program for minority businesses. The order did not prescribe specific goals, but directed the Secretary of Commerce to develop and coordinate activities at the federal, state and local levels which aimed at promoting minority business development. The head of each federal department, or his or her designated representative, was made responsible for submitting reports to the Commerce Secretary on the department's budget, plans and programs to assist minority businesses. These activities led to the establishment of the Office of Minority Business Enterprise.

To increase awards to minority businesses on federal contracts, section 8(a) of the Small Business Act was used. This section authorizes the SBA to enter into contracts with federal agencies and in turn award these contracts to small businesses. The 8(a) provision became one of the primary means of increasing the use of minorities in federal procurement.

In fiscal year 1969, $8.9 million was awarded under the 8(a) program. By 1971 this had grown to $64.5 million, and by 1973 it reached $208 million. Between 1968 and 1977, $2.2 billion was awarded under this program.[2]

The Public Works Employment Act of 1977[3] and the 1978 Omnibus Small Business Act[4] established percentage goals in procurement for minority-owned firms for the first time. The acts required at least 10 percent of all federal grants for local public works projects to be expended with minority businesses, and directed the Secretary of Commerce, in cooperation with federal departments and agencies, to develop comprehensive minority enterprise programs and institute specific goals for minority firms in federal procurement. Monitoring and evaluation procedures were established to assess the performance against these goals. A new subcontracting program was introduced under section 8(d) of the Small Business Act that required recipients of federal prime contracts exceeding $1 million for the construction of a public facility to establish percentage goals for the use of minority subcontractors. In 1981, minority-owned firms received 3.4 percent of all federal procurement expenditures. By 1994 they received 8.3 percent or $14.4 billion.

Affirmative action grows among local governments

In January 1974, Maynard Jackson became the first black Mayor of the City of Atlanta. Soon afterwards, black entrepreneurs got an opportunity to break into the contracting operations of the city in a significant way. Impatient with racial injustice, Jackson demanded the immediate implementation of affirmative action policies in employment and minority business contracting. The speed with which Jackson adopted these policies led his opponents to label him "arrogant" and to accuse him of lacking a spirit of compromise. But Jackson's policies constituted a watershed for black businesses in Atlanta and in the nation.

The minority business program established by Jackson opened new markets and created new opportunities for black entrepreneurs. The access to large-scale public contracts created by these programs allowed black-owned businesses to diversify into non-traditional industries. In turn, this diversification helped to catalyze the emergence of a new cadre of black entrepreneurs in Atlanta.

Prior to Jackson's first term as mayor, compromise and gradualism governed race relations in Atlanta.[5] Clarence Stone notes that during the South's most die-hard segregationist era, Atlanta's Mayors William Hartsfield (1937 to 1940, and June 1942 to 1961) and Ivan Allen, Jr. (1962 to 1969) formed alliances between downtown business interests and the black political elite to ensure that racial progress occurred in Atlanta through "moderation and negotiated gradualism."[6] One of the most influential figures among the black political elite was John Wesley Dobb, the maternal grandfather of Maynard Jackson.

Jackson's family had deep roots in the political tradition of Atlanta, but Maynard was not given to abiding by all of its traditions. In fact, during his run for vice-mayor, he was accused of "leap-frogging" the establishment, of failing to first clear his candidacy, and of failing to make the "Stations of the Cross."[7] At the young age of thirty-one, Jackson became vice mayor. Four years later, he captured the office of Mayor (1974 to 1982 and 1990 to 1994). Having bucked tradition in the black establishment, he used his new position to attack racist traditions in city government.

Gradualism on the issue of racial equality did not sit well with the new mayor. To Jackson, it was clear that past policies had virtually no impact on black business development. The Annual Reports of the Office of Contract Compliance at the city indicate that in 1973, the year Jackson was elected Mayor, blacks received their first contract from the city. Their total amounted to just $41,800 of the $33.1 million in contracts awarded that year. A study of the city's contracting history with blacks and other minorities reveals that insidious forms of discrimination were practiced until the 1970s. The city once maintained separate job qualification registers for blacks and whites, separate water fountains at City Hall, and did not provide blacks with knowledge of bid opportunities.[8]

Mayor Jackson made a frontal assault on the city's racial traditions:

> When I became Mayor of this city in 1974 my first order of business was to use every resource at my disposal to end the pervasive racial and gender discrimination which I knew to exist in the City of Atlanta. We didn't need to conduct a study or hold extensive public hearings to know that this city would not continue to grow with the majority of its population shut out of the commercial marketplace. . . . Let me be clear, MBE's [Minority Business Enterprises] in the City of Atlanta did not improve their status until the first term of my administration. Without concerted governmental action there would have been no improvement.[9]

Affirmative action in city contracting is the tool that Jackson used to create opportunity for black entrepreneurs. His opponents had indeed characterized him correctly. Jackson was uncompromising as he prepared to implement the boldest minority business affirmative action plan ever undertaken in the nation. He targeted the newly planned $1 billion Hartsfield International Airport. His goal was to have 25 percent of the awards for construction-related contracts go to minority-owned businesses. This meant that for the first time black contractors could move out of small-scale residential construction and repairs as well as small-scale commercial construction. Instead, they could now engage in large-scale public works projects. These projects also required architectural and engineering services, construction management, and public relations and related contracting expertise. The affirmative action plan caused a significant change in the character of the city's black-owned businesses.

The ability to diversify away from personal service and retail activities into non-traditional industries is the most important legacy of minority business affirmative action policies. New market opportunities meant faster growth possibilities, greater profitability and increased employment capacity. Black-owned firms that did not receive city contracts directly benefited nonetheless because affirmative action hastened the decline of racial stereotypes, improved networks between black and white entrepreneurs, and encouraged private companies to emulate public sector affirmative action initiatives.

The opportunities created by Atlanta's program attracted blacks out of corporate-sector management, administrative and executive positions and into entrepreneurial careers. These opportunities also encouraged black entrepreneurs across the country to migrate to the city. Jackson's bold step had such an enormous psychological impact on the nation's black business sector that Atlanta was soon nicknamed, "the black Mecca." More than 100 cities across the country followed Atlanta's lead. For ten years, the city's program was the model and standard against which other programs were measured.

Atlanta's minority business plan was the first local program with a significant minority goal that was not tied to a federal mandate. It predated by two years the Public Works Employment Act of 1977 that established federal set-asides.

Mayor Jackson's affirmative action initiative grew out of the 1974 "Atlanta Plan." This plan was designed in response to the Presidential Executive Order 11246 and was intended to ensure equal employment opportunity in all city activities. In 1975, Jackson extended the scope of the plan by an administrative order that mandated the use of minority contractors on the construction of the airport. Jackson interpreted this mandate as a way of achieving the goals of Title VII of the Civil Rights Act of 1964 and the Equal Employment Opportunity Act of 1972.

Opposition to the plan was intense because the planned airport was one of the largest capital construction projects in the South.

Dave Miller, the individual tapped by Jackson to manage airport development, recounted in a conversation with the author the tense racial atmosphere that surrounded Jackson's decision. On one occasion, Miller noted, a white contractor shouted at the Mayor in an open meeting that "Niggers don't fly airplanes, what do they know about building airports." Still, the plan went forward. Race relations grew more tense when, in addition to the airport mandate, Jackson threatened to withdraw city funds from local banks unless they took immediate steps to elevate minorities to executive level positions.[10]

In 1976, the city council formally adopted the "Midfield Resolution" which mandated that 25 percent of funds expended on the design and construction of the new airport should go to minorities as joint venture partners, prime contractors or subcontractors. Soon afterwards, this minority business initiative was extended by an executive order to cover all city contracting.

In 1982, these policies were formally adopted by the city council in a minority and female business enterprise ordinance. This ordinance required minority and female business participation on all airport concessions, public construction projects, consultant services and lease agreements awarded by the city with a value of $25,000 or more.

Minority business utilization by the City of Atlanta increased substantially following the implementation of the plan. According to published reports, total minority procurement was 0.13 percent in 1973, 3 percent in 1974, 14.3 percent in 1975, 19.9 percent in 1976 and 24.1 percent in 1977. By the end of Jackson's first term in 1978 the city boasted of having achieved 38.5 percent minority participation. Jackson's policies increased minority procurement significantly, but actual percentages were below the claims made by the Contract Compliance Office. For one thing, the program did not cover the procurement of commodities and supplies, but focused mainly on construction contracting and related contractual services. In an independent examination of contracts awarded between 1979 and 1989, the author determined that minorities and white women received $191 million or 15.5 percent of all dollars awarded during this period. This included 11.4 percent of all prime contracts, 17.5 percent of all subcontracts, and 27.6 percent of all joint ventures. These awards went to 359 different firms owned by minorities and white women. Of this total, 309 were black-owned firms. An examination of bid activity indicates that blacks submitted 29 percent of all construction bids during this period.[11]

In November 1987, the Georgia Supreme Court issued a ruling that affirmed the constitutionality of the City of Atlanta's minority business program. The decision was in response to an earlier suit. The court held that the city's program was consistent with Georgia's Constitution and was narrowly tailored to remedy the effects of past discrimination. However, when the U.S. Supreme Court rendered its decision on the Croson case in January 1989, the Georgia Supreme Court on appeal cited Croson almost verbatim to invalidate Atlanta's program.

The court argued that the success of minority inclusion in contracting up to 1982 made the program unnecessary.[12] In addition, it ruled that Atlanta's program did not conform to the "strict scrutiny" standard. It considered three criteria in forming its opinion: whether the legislation to enact the program is within the power of the City of Atlanta; whether there is convincing evidence of prior discrimination sufficient to provide the city with a compelling interest in using a race-conscious remedy; and whether the minority business participation program is narrowly tailored to address the effects of past discrimination. While not ruling on the first criterion, the court ruled that the program did not conform to the requirements of the second and third criteria, and was therefore invalid.

To meet the "strict scrutiny" standard Andrew Young, Mayor of Atlanta from 1982 to 1990, decided to do whatever was necessary to comply with the Croson decision. This meant spending over a half million dollars in consultants' fees to determine whether the city had engaged in discriminatory practices in the past either directly or indirectly by awarding contracts to firms that discriminated. Former Federal Reserve Board Governor Andrew F. Brimmer and former Secretary of Labor Raymond Marshall directed the consulting team. The team included over a dozen other consultants and the final report contains eight parts and totals 1,069 pages.[13] Testifying before the city council upon the re-enactment of the program, Maynard Jackson, who was re-elected Mayor following Young's last term, made the following statement:

It is particularly ironic that we hold these hearings on April 5, 1991. One day after we pause to mourn the 23rd anniversary of the assassination of Dr. Martin Luther King, Jr., we are forced to continue to prove, with the particularity demanded by the courts, the existence of discrimination which is empirically evident to anyone who cares to look. I protest that and testify, therefore, under protest. Despite my belief, stated previously, the City of Atlanta should not be forced to pay $517,650 to prove an unjust past that is common knowledge. Despite our disappointment with the posture of the courts, we have taken every step required under the rulings of the U.S. Supreme Court in City of Richmond v. J.A. Croson, and of the Georgia Supreme Court in American Subcontractors Association v. City of Atlanta, to make certain that the City of Atlanta can resume our efforts to ensure that all of our citizens are given an equal opportunity to participate in the commercial life of our city.[14]

During the 1980s dozens of cities followed Atlanta's lead. By the mid-1980s there were over 200 local and state programs nation-wide.[15] But the Croson Decision altered this. Following this case, minority business programs across the country were sued. Many were forced out of existence, while others were modified significantly. To operate these programs cities had to spend about a quarter of a million dollars on a disparity study to meet the "strict scrutiny" standard required by the Croson Decision. Some cities chose to do so, others did not or could not afford to.

Despite legal setbacks, the first wave of affirmative action programs (that is those up to the 1989 Croson Decision) planted the seeds for the emergence of a new generation of black business owners. Although most programs emphasized public works contracting, other types of procurement opportunities were made available also. For example, between 1992 and 1995, firms receiving prime construction contracts in Atlanta awarded $163,477,896 in subcontracts. Of this amount, $72.5 million went to black-owned firms, but not all of this was in construction, $13 million was for the procurement of commodities and supplies, $7.5 million was for the procurement of general services and $4.8 million was for the procurement of professional services. Added to this, millions of dollars were awarded directly in the procurement of goods and supplies.[16] Between 1992 and 1995, 816 black-owned firms either received awards from the City of Atlanta, bid on awards, or were certified by the Compliance Office. Of this number, 31.2 percent of firms were in construction related services, 10.5 percent were in architectural and engineering services, 23.3 percent were in professional services, 10.7 percent were in general services, and 24.3 percent were goods suppliers. The important point is that minority business programs opened opportunities in a cross-section of industries.

The effectiveness of these programs varied from city to city. Some cities instituted programs with provisions that were never implemented. In cities where effective programs operated, they were usually challenged legally. The Associated General Contractors of America initiated many of the earlier suits.

Along with the legal challenges, opponents of affirmative action promoted negative images of the programs and seized upon their problems to undermine public confidence in them. The projected image of these programs was one where front companies posing as minority-owned firms dominated and only a few "well heeled" minority businesses benefited. It was argued that the programs drove the cost of procurement up significantly and made awards to firms that were incapable of performing. To popularize these stereotypes, every negative incident involving a minority procurement plan was well publicized and the incident was used to make generalizations about all affirmative action procurement programs.

Earlier we noted that between 1979 and 1989, Atlanta awarded contracts to 359 different minority firms. Yet, the perception is that only a few large minority-owned firms received awards. In truth, the procurement records reveal that awards are more concentrated among the city's white-owned firms than they are among minority-owned firms. Nevertheless minority business programs are singled out for ridicule.

A few years back, terrible abuses occurred among the nation's major defense contractors and among some of the nation's leading universities. Just recently, the government released information indicating that some major contractors were charging as much as $58.00 for a screw. The government normally handles these kinds of abuses by penalizing the abusers, establishing more stringent guidelines, and increasing its compliance and monitoring activities. But when abuses occur within federal set-aside programs, large contingents of Congressmen seek their termination. Clearly, this is a double standard.

How opportunity makes a difference

The rapid growth of black-owned businesses in the Atlanta metropolitan area is well documented. Earlier we noted that the metro area's black-owned businesses nearly doubled between 1987 and 1992, increasing from 11,804 to 23,488 in just five years. The main factor that drives the increase in the number of black-owned businesses is income growth in the metropolitan area. Table 1.1a reports data on the twenty-five metropolitan areas with the largest number of black-owned firms. It gives the percent change in per capita income (that is income per person) between 1982 and 1992. It also gives the number of black-owned businesses per one-thousand black residents in the metro area (that is the black business rate), the percent change in the black business rate between 1982 and 1992, and the percent change in the total population for the same period. A regression analysis was conducted using these data to see if the percent change in income and the percent change

Table 1.1a Selected changes in twenty-five metropolitan areas with the largest number of black-owned firms, 1982–92

Metropolitan area	Change in per capita income	Black business per 1,000 blacks (1992)	Change in black business rate	Change in total population
Atlanta, GA	84.1%	31.9	124.8%	34.0%
Baltimore, MD	78.8%	20.3	76.9%	34.0%
Baton Rouge, LA	61.4%	19.3	50.4%	14.0%
Columbia, SC	88.4%	23.7	87.4%	10.0%
Columbus, OH	81.0%	23.7	46.5%	18.0%
Dallas–Fort Worth, TX	53.9%	20.5	9.2%	4.0%
Dayton, OH	75.6%	20.1	41.3%	15.0%
Greensboro–Winston Salem–Highpoint	85.11%	26.0	103.1%	5.0%
Houston, TX	47.3%	28.3	22.5%	10.0%
Indianapolis, IN	84.5 %	23.2	45.2%	32.0%
Jackson, MS	70.1%	22.4	88.8%	13.0%
Kansas City, MO–KS	68.3%	19.8	38.1%	1.0%
Little Rock, AR	77.9%	20.1	71.0%	8.0%
Los Angeles–Long Beach, CA	56.0%	26.5	6.3%	21.0%
Louisville, KY	82.8%	20.1	62.1%	32.0%
Nashville–Davidson, TN	91.1%	25.4	76.2%	9.0%
Norfolk–Virginia Beach–Portsmouth, VA	65.7%	18.7	−0.3%	40.0%
Raleigh–Durham, NC	96.9%	30.5	101.4%	11.0%
Richmond, VA	78.0%	22.8	27.8%	21.0%
Sacramento, CA	73.7%	26.8	10.5%	3.0%
San Diego, CA	63.8%	24.0	23.4%	27.0%
St. Louis, MO	74.8%	17.3	50.8%	23.0%
Tampa, FL	70.8%	21.3	80.0%	12.0%
Washington DC–MD–VA	81.8%	36.5	65.7%	11.0%
West Palm Beach, FL	100.1%	25.7	96.8%	17.0%

Source: U.S. Department of Commerce, Bureau of the Census, *Survey of Minority-owned Business Enterprises: Black*; and Census of the Population.

Table 1.1b Statistics for urban black-owned businesses, 1982–92

City/state	Total firms			Total sales (000)			Total employment			Date affirmative action plan initiated	Plan coverage	Goal of plan	Change in no. of businesses	
	1982	1987	1992	1982	1987	1992	1982	1987	1992				1982–92	1987–92
Akron, OH	628	679	940	10,556	14,034	20,922	164	140	312	1984	Construction	15%	50%	38%
Anchorage, AK	312	347	518	11,907	11,334	32,321	217	161	832	1984	Construction	10%	66%	49%
Atlanta, GA	3,496	3,869	5,762	238,549	290,702	280,701	4,162	3,230	3,299	1982	Goods & services	25%	65%	49%
Augusta, GA	294	272	391	18,518	12,326	12,736	472	187	343	1982	(NA)	(NG)	33%	44%
Austin, TX	815	1,111	1,579	19,704	31,689	45,026	397	731	871	1982	Construction	8%	94%	42%
Baltimore, MD	4,077	5,044	7,542	241,024	165,350	233,164	2,411	1,898	2,409	1982	Construction contracts	25%	85%	50%
Baton Rouge, LA	1,177	1,196	1,791	45,022	56,261	67,623	700	629	680	1986	Construction	10%	52%	50%
Birmingham, AL	1,145	1,437	2,105	47,107	48,281	77,364	892	778	1,103	1980	Procurement	13%	84%	46%
Boston, MA	1,214	1,860	2,583	59,224	86,220	182,525	(D)	928	(D)	1987	Goods & services	23%	113%	39%
Buffalo, NY	717	735	1,011	25,993	31,484	36,321	697	345	639	(NA)	Construction	10%	41%	38%
Camden, NJ	264	270	356	5,771	9,103	28,514	41	116	906	1983	(NA)	(NG)	35%	32%
Charleston, SC	490	456	703	14,838	15,825	26,251	218	234	629	1979	(NA)	(NG)	43%	54%
Charlotte, NC	1,308	1,880	3,216	48,470	75,885	123,654	576	945	951	1983	Construction grants	10%	146%	71%
Chattanooga, TN	485	584	793	17,712	16,110	23,502	(D)	211	519	(NA)	Construction grants	12%	64%	36%
Cincinnati, OH	1,636	1,753	2,431	45,389	58,008	94,881	642	901	1,166	1983	Construction	15%	49%	39%
Cleveland, OH	2,407	2,359	2,943	131,494	107,098	125,170	1,492	1,516	1,247	1984	Construction	30%	22%	25%
Columbia, SC	629	743	1,225	16,104	41,016	–	259	622	(D)	1986	(NA)	(NA)	95%	65%
Columbus, GA	618	866	1,255	16,151	43,707	98,384	257	1,115	922	1984	Procurement	4%	103%	45%
Columbus, OH	1,906	2,301	3,314	37,419	64,996	188,630	604	1,074	2,265	1983	Construction contracts	10%	74%	44%

City										Year				
Dallas, TX	4,883	5,633	7,071	134,357	157,962	330,354	1,875	1,992	5,191	1987	Construction contracts	20%	45%	26%
Dayton, OH	908	879	1,122	20,123	33,134	31,716	336	644	432	(NA)	Construction contracts	20%	24%	28%
Denver, CO	1,325	1,383	1,916	53,076	52,155	121,622	664	438	1,636	(NA)	Construction contracts	20%	45%	39%
Detroit, MI	6,798	7,116	9,275	272,405	258,375	486,092	2,877	3,861	4,528	(NA)	(NA)		36%	30%
Durham, NC	693	936	1,589	69,929	27,506	43,805	1,808	512	649	1984	Services & construction	28%	129%	70%
East Orange, NJ	659	938	1,132	21,386	26,470	35,936	227	168	336	1982	Construction contracts	25%	72%	21%
El Paso, TX	266	305	503	8,308	19,632	16,570	(D)	814	210	1985	Construction	20%	89%	65%
Evanston, IL	337	451	679	6,963	13,120	43,182	81	99	578	1973	(NA)	(NG)	101%	51%
Flint, MI	634	683	960	26,481	21,018	22,309	218	230	259	(NA)	Construction contracts	18%	51%	41%
Fort Lauderdale, FL	472	620	643	12,201	34,337	26,200	194	365	267	1986	(NA)	(NG)	36%	4%
Fort Wayne, IN	293	350	544	9,445	22,584	25,177	197	381	(D)	1984	Procurement	10%	86%	55%
Fresno, CA	306	359	486	9,377	14,403	21,725	133	191	274	1986	Construction	25%	59%	35%
Gardena, CA	322	316	488	6,905	10,534	31,940	65	70	187	1984	Procurement	10%	52%	54%
Gary, IN	1,103	1,051	1,274	49,005	77,456	84,777	171	894	854	(NA)	(NA)	(NA)	16%	21%
Grand Rapids, MI	252	312	494	7,419	13,719	16,594	84	107	144	1982	Construction contracts	10%	96%	58%
Greensboro, NC	897	1,094	1,617	22,460	30,751	45,201	312	461	915	(NA)	Construction	10%	80%	48%
Hampton, VA	660	936	1,179	17,110	61,310	22,729	189	531	353	1985	(NA)	(NG)	79%	26%
Harrisburg, PA	258	328	384	7,193	12,817	10,541	96	232	144	1982	Construction	15%	49%	17%
Hartford, CT	436	526	751	23,570	32,758	26,551	236	480	218	1983	Construction contracts	10%	72%	43%
Houston, TX	10,019	10,025	13,592	283,724	288,897	537,490	2,470	2,561	6,191	(NA)	Construction	10%	36%	36%
Jackson, MS	1,251	1,738	2,560	38,093	71,603	93,616	593	1,235	1,623	1985	(NA)	(NA)	105%	47%
Jacksonville, FL	1,703	1,967	2,507	53,755	80,913	112,765	1,031	1,156	1,710	1984	Goods & services	10%	47%	27%
Kansas City, KS	601	670	778	28,776	29,239	19,688	246	775	(D)	(NA)	Contracts	10%	29%	16%
Kansas City, MO	1,552	1,812	2,243	60,594	78,673	84,997	767	1,568	1,565	(NA)	Construction	16%	45%	24%
Lake Charles, LA	416	490	644	10,780	13,876	16,124	168	185	(D)	1980	Procurement	10%	55%	31%
Los Angeles, CA	12,197	11,607	15,371	459,754	721,958	2,628,903	5,727	5,527	13,138	1983	Construction	16%	26%	32%
Louisville, KY	973	1,097	1,465	44,056	32,882	94,997	1,294	567	1,038	1983	Credit-MBE bids	15%	51%	34%

Table 1.1b Statistics for urban black-owned businesses, 1982–92 (continued)

City/state	Total firms			Total sales (000)			Total employment			Date affirmative action plan initiated	Plan coverage	Goal of plan	Change in no. of businesses	
	1982	1987	1992	1982	1987	1992	1982	1987	1992				1982–92	1987–92
Macon, GA	393	663	932	9,925	52,225	27,694	193	478	417	1983	(NA)	(NG)	137%	41%
Memphis, TN	3,119	4,225	5,662	139,902	147,861	183,665	2,164	2,337	2,257	(NA)	Program pending	(NA)	82%	34%
Miami, FL	1,142	1,164	2,155	59,358	78,989	86,584	676	852	876	1985	Goods and services	50%	89%	85%
Milwaukee, WI	1,516	1,741	2,423	59,807	73,002	176,966	664	870	2,112	1987	All projects	15%	60%	39%
Minneapolis, MN	554	603	1,114	43,970	44,147	68,217	823	773	964	(NA)	Construction supplies	10%	101%	85%
Monroe, LA	270	350	429	8,117	35,512	16,369	165	231	90	1986	Goods & services	10%	59%	23%
New Haven, CT	333	448	570	37,705	15,348	14,608	142	127	119	1963	Construction projects	15%	71%	27%
New York City, NY	17,350	25,256	35,120	641,187	1,065,032	1,466,994	8,010	8,727	8,779	(NA)	Construction contracts	10%	102%	39%
Newark, NJ	918	1,231	1,500	60,781	124,118	144,114	1,067	901	1,200	1984	Construction	25%	63%	22%
Norfolk, VA	922	1,165	1,248	45,222	46,546	35,911	1,069	872	621				35%	7%
Oakland, CA	3,633	3,445	4,282	181,179	137,159	215,057	2,861	1,711	2,612	1980	DOT funded	30%	18%	24%
Omaha, NE	538	633	975	32,901	21,899	47,110	(D)	469	(D)	1985	Construction	20%	81%	54%
Orlando, FL	427	463	811	13,068	29,800	37,030	163	425	647	(NA)	Construction/services/supplies	18%	90%	75%
Pasadena, CA	573	642	901	13,227	23,341	35,260	125	206	301	1980	(NA)	(NG)	57%	40%
Philadelphia, PA	5,017	5,540	7,183	215,337	255,907	549,414	2,316	2,474	5,962	1984	Construction and services	15%	43%	30%
Phoenix, AZ	685	776	1,204	22,352	47,150	64,438	330	937	617	(NA)	All areas	12%	76%	55%
Plainfield, NJ	384	519	659	12,154	13,795	15,088	452	178	112	1981	Contracts	25%	72%	27%
Portsmouth, VA	614	687	770	10,421	16,658	16,168	133	296	232	(NA)	All projects	(NG)	25%	12%
Raleigh, NC	655	984	1,619	16,717	37,804	56,653	298	721	718	(NA)	Construction—SW Raleigh	9%	147%	65%

City														
Richmond, VA	1,563	1,838	2,630	45,360	57,420	95,777	815	821	1,596	1983	Construction	30%	68%	43%
Richmond, CA	623	660	874	29,402	25,465	29,703	351	407	405	(NA)	Construction projects	10%	40%	32%
Rochester, NY	498	655	926	17,999	21,001	23,699	244	366	365	1985	Procurement	20%	86%	41%
Sacramento, CA	843	809	1,313	12,424	21,652	42,511	150	226	359	1980	Construction	14%	56%	62%
San Antonio, TX	989	1,273	1,477	25,597	41,865	68,583	363	602	1,073	1984	Public works	30%	49%	16%
San Francisco, CA	1,980	1,965	2,230	80,193	99,296	220,799	1,264	1,209	2,005	1983	(NA)	13%	13%	13%
San Jose, CA	998	961	1,351	30,516	36,739	48,252	515	295	567	1986	(NA)	(NG)	35%	41%
Seattle, WA	1,063	1,040	1,569	36,011	37,997	83,569	719	722	1,498	1980	Construction & consulting	21%	48%	51%
Shreveport, LA	827	1,018	1,216	27,063	29,054	32,066	477	385	697	1984	Construction	10%	47%	19%
Springfield, MA	265	429	515	8,441	13,748	13,058	69	105	95	1981	Construction contracts	5%	94%	20%
St Petersburg, FL	566	788	919	17,889	29,158	26,528	219	343	198	(NA)	Construction	5%	62%	17%
St. Louis, MO	2,164	2,235	2,481	89,543	83,826	98,443	1,307	1,255	1,060	1979	Contracts	10%	15%	11%
Stockton, CA	260	299	374	6,478	11,901	15,855	79	139	180	1971	Procurement	15%	44%	25%
Tacoma, WA	287	287	442	5,451	10,719	13,144	72	101	190	1982	Contracts & purchasing	15%	54%	54%
Tallahassee, FL	310	501	799	12,885	41,893	33,944	158	597	371	1985	Contracts – $100,000+	15%	158%	59%
Tampa, FL	606	800	1,118	20,263	88,342	70,478	392	695	845	1981	(NA)	(NG)	84%	40%
Tulsa, OK	680	738	1,114	12,368	26,533	31,751	139	379	431	1986	(NA)	(NG)	64%	51%
Tucson, AZ	259	247	448	7,863	7,592	10,521	150	126	137	(NA)	Construction	17%	73%	81%
Washington, DC	8,966	8,275	10,111	268,488	411,941	451,861	3,417	4,085	4,277	1981	Construction	35%	13%	22%
Wilmington, DE	332	377	544	12,485	16,991	41,932	223	286	1,488	(NA)	Construction	15%	64%	44%
Winston-Salem, NC	513	703	1,061	15,052	26,305	34,285	302	399	324	(NA)	Construction	(NG)	107%	51%
Wichita, KS	588	601	746	18,068	71,164	18,709	(D)	335	(D)	1983	Construction	10%	27%	24%
Youngstown, OH	330	337	451	7,650	7,910	17,300	113	113	298	1980	Construction	20%	37%	34%

Source: U.S. Department of Commerce, Bureau of the Census, Survey of Minority-owned Business Enterprises. Data on program goals from minority Business Enterprise Legal Defense and Education Fund, "Report on the Minority Business Programs of State and Local Government" (1988).

Notes: Where (D) denotes withheld by government to avoid disclosing data for individual companies; (NA) plan coverage, specific goal or specific date plan initiated, unknown; (NG) no goal adopted.

in population influence the percent change in the black business rate. The results indicate that among these metro areas, when per capita income increases by 10 percent, the black business rate increases by 18.9 percent. Population change was not found to be significant in influencing the black business rate.[17]

A similar analysis was conducted for all metropolitan areas that had more than 200 black-owned businesses in 1982. There were 103 such areas. In this case the regression sought to determine if the percent change in per capita income and population influences the percent change in the number of black-owned businesses in metropolitan areas. The time frame for this analysis was 1982 to 1987 and the results are similar to those in Table 1.1a in that income change is found to influence the growth of black-owned businesses. Specifically, a 10 percent increase in per capita income causes the percent change in businesses to increase by 5.6 percent. The percent change in population was still not statistically significant.[18]

We also used the data to determine if the presence of a race-based affirmative action program, along with changes in per capita income and population, influences the growth, revenue and employment of black-owned businesses in cities. To conduct this analysis we selected all cities with at least 200 black-owned businesses in 1982. Table 1.1b lists the information recorded for these cities. It includes the number of black businesses in 1982, 1987 and 1992, their combined revenue and employment and whether they had an affirmative action plan prior to 1987. This cut off was used because it is the census period that predates the 1989 Croson Decision. Following that decision, numerous programs were struck down in court. The table indicates the area of contracting and procurement covered by the plan, the date it was enacted and the percentage goal of the plan. The latter information was obtained from a report of the Minority Business Enterprise Legal Defense and Education Fund.[19]

There were eighty-eight cities with at least 200 black-owned businesses in 1982. Of this number of cities, 76 percent implemented affirmative action plans prior to 1987. The average year that plans were implemented is 1983. Between 1987 and 1992 the average increase in the number of businesses in cities with affirmative action plans was 41 percent; the average increase in cities without plans was 36 percent. Between 1982 and 1992, the average increase in the number of black-owned businesses in cities with plans was 65 percent; in cities without plans the average increase was 61 percent. Although the growth rate is greater in cities with affirmative action programs than in cities without programs, the difference of about 5 percentage points is not statistically significant.

Unfortunately, there is a significant limitation in attempting to use census data to conduct this type of analysis. Specifically, we cannot evaluate the change in revenue and employment of black-owned businesses because census data from the Survey of Minority-owned Business Enterprises (SMOBE) do not include information on 1120 Subchapter C corporations but only on 1120 S Corporations.[20] The former are considered regular corporations. Regular corporations are most prominent in affirmative action programs. For example, 57.9 percent of all businesses certified to participate in programs offered by the City of Atlanta and Fulton County are corporations, and 72.6 percent of these corporations are 1120 C corporations.[21] This same trend prevails in other minority business programs across the country. Usually, firms registered in these programs have much greater revenues and employment capacities, and the majority of the corporations are 1120 C corporations. But census data on minority-owned businesses do not include C corporations. For this reason, it is not feasible to use census data to measure the influence of affirmative action plans on the revenue and employment of black-owned firms. Ironically, these are the areas where these programs have had their greatest impact. Specifically, *the most important effect of affirmative action programs on black-owned businesses is the changes they have brought about in the diversification of these businesses, in their access to new markets, and in their revenue and employment capacity.*

For example, Table 1.2 lists the twenty detailed industries within which the largest number of the 1,451 minority-owned firms, registered with various public agencies in Atlanta, can be classified. These very diverse industries reflect the contracting and procurement opportunities available at public agencies in Atlanta. While general building contracting has the largest number of firms (8.7 percent), it is followed by computer and data processing (5.6 percent), engineering and architectural services (4.9 percent), services to buildings (4.7 percent), business services (4.7 percent), and management and public relations (4.6 percent).

Social benefits of minority business programs

Do black-owned firms generate employment opportunities for blacks and do they make a difference in low-income communities? Until recently, data limitations made these two questions difficult

Table 1.2 Twenty detailed industries with the largest percentage of
minority and women-owned firms, Atlanta metropolitan area,
1994 (total number of firms = 1,451)

Standard Industrial Classification	Industry	No. of firms	% of total
150	General building contractors	123	8.71%
737	Computer/data processing services	80	5.67%
871	Engineering/architectural services	70	4.96%
734	Services to buildings	67	4.75%
739	Business services, necessary	65	4.60%
874	Management and public relations	65	4.60%
170	Special trades contractors	56	3.97%
508	Machinery, equipment, wholesale	54	3.82%
275	Commercial printing	47	3.33%
506	Electrical goods, wholesale	44	3.12%
172	Painting and paper hanging	40	2.83%
173	Electrical work	36	2.55%
174	Masonry, stonework and plastering	33	2.34%
736	Personnel supply services	33	2.34%
502	Furniture and home furnishings	26	1.84%
420	Trucking and warehousing	24	1.70%
730	Business services	24	1.70%
731	Advertising	24	1.70%
738	Miscellaneous business services	23	1.63%
171	Plumbing, heating and air	21	1.49%

Source: Combined minority business vendor lists of the Atlanta Business League, City of
Atlanta, Atlanta Public Schools, Fulton County, Georgia Minority Supplier
Development Council, Dekalb County, Grady Health Systems, Metropolitan Atlanta
Rapid Transit System. Comprehensive list compiled by Thomas D. Boston.

to answer precisely. But new studies are providing convincing
evidence that black-owned firms are about eight times more likely
to employ blacks than are firms owned by non-blacks.

Tim Bates argues that promoting black business development is
important because these businesses generate jobs for blacks. He
finds that whether minority-owned businesses are located in urban
poverty areas or elsewhere, they still employ black workers. By
contrast, black workers are a distinct minority in white-owned
firms, even when such firms are located in distressed urban areas
that are predominantly black.[22]

In 1994, there were 722 black-owned firms located in the
Atlanta metropolitan area and certified by the City of Atlanta and
Fulton County's minority business programs. Firm-level data was
collected on these companies. These data also included background
information on their owners. Tables 1.3 through 1.7 profile these

firms and their owners. Table 1.3 indicates that 57.9 percent of these firms are corporations. Nationally, only 4 percent of black-owned firms are corporations. The average revenue of these firms was $606,203.00.[23] Average revenue for corporations was $855,548, average revenue for partnerships was $527,049 and for proprietorships it was $153,209. It is well recognized that minority business programs typically attract some of the most successful black-owned businesses in the local area. For example, while 4 percent of all black-owned businesses nationally are corporations, 57.9 percent of the black-owned businesses in Atlanta's program are corporations. Similarly, while the average revenue of all black-owned firms in the metropolitan area in 1992 was $44,668, the average revenue of firms registered with the city as program was $606,208.

Table 1.4 indicates that firms owned by black men gross $663,110 annually while firms owned by black women gross $388,183 annually. Male firms have 4.8 times more total assets than black women-owned firms but only 2.2 times their equity and 1.1 times their net profits. Table 1.5 reveals that the greatest annual earnings are generated in manufacturing ($1,801,458) and whole-sale ($1,311,943). In 1993, these 722 black-owned firms generated $437,682,176 in revenue and employed 6,410 workers; 77 percent of these workers were black.

The educational attainment of black business owners registered in these two programs is given in Table 1.6. It reveals that 62.3 percent have completed college or better while 22.2 percent have completed graduate education. The annual revenue of business owners, corresponding to their educational attainment, is given in Table 1.7. Business owners not advancing beyond the high school level gross $131,974 annually while individuals with some graduate education gross over $2.5 million annually.

Table 1.8 provides information on the industry distribution,

Table 1.3 Legal form of organization by revenue, 1992–3

Legal form	Mean revenue	Median revenue	Number	% of total
Annual revenue				
Proprietorship	$153,209	$50,118	278	38.5%
Partnership	$527,049	$128,885	26	3.6%
Corporation	$855,548	$168,746	418	57.9%
Table total	$606,208	$108,168	722	100%

Source: Primary data collected by Thomas D. Boston from City of Atlanta and Fulton County Certification Records.

Table 1.4 Financial data on successful black-owned firms in Atlanta, 1992–3

Gender	Mean revenue	Median
Annual revenue		
Male	$663,110	$116,309
Female	$388,183	$64,925
Table total	$606,208	$108,168
Net profits		
Male	$16,847	$3,563
Female	$15,043	$2,999
Table total	$16,464	$3,528
Current assets		
Male	$293,111	$42,950
Female	$105,382	$21,736
Table total	$252,252	$36,564
Total assets		
Male	$903,687	$96,852
Female	$187,125	$51,550
Table total	$744,674	$87,272
Equity		
Male	$191,299	$32,244
Female	$86,860	$40,949
Table total	$168,897	$35,055

Source: Primary data collected by Thomas D. Boston from City of Atlanta and Fulton County Certification Records.

Table 1.5 Average revenue by Standard Industrial Classification, 1992

Industry	Mean revenue	Median revenue
Annual revenue		
General building construction	$685,906	$83,165
Heavy construction	ND	ND
Special trades construction	$291,942	$94,666
Manufacturing	$1,801,458	$77,878
Transportation and utilities	$765,184	$168,746
Wholesale and retail	$1,311,943	$243,320
Finance, insurance, real estate	$540,078	$95,806
Services (excl. engineer/management)	$473,738	$69,006
Engineering and management services	$608,921	$123,993
Services not elsewhere classified	ND	ND
Table total	$606,208	$108,168

Source: Primary data collected by Thomas D. Boston from City of Atlanta and Fulton County Certification Records.
ND = not disclosed.

Table 1.6 Educational attainment of successful black entrepreneurs in Atlanta, 1992–3

Educational attainment	Number	% of total
High school graduate	24	4.6%
Technical or vocational degree	64	12.4%
Some college (including associate degree)	107	20.7%
College graduate	184	35.5%
Some graduate school	24	4.6%
Graduate or professional degree	115	22.2%

Source: \Primary data collected by Thomas D. Boston from City of Atlanta and Fulton County Certification Records.

Table 1.7 Revenue and educational characteristics of owners in Atlanta, 1992–3

Educational attainment	Mean revenue	Median revenue
High school graduate	$131,974	$83,164
Technical or vocational degree	$231,446	$122,799
Some college (including associate degree)	$279,050	$43,874
College graduate	$623,431	$94,666
Some graduate school	$2,544,474	$683,832
Graduate or professional degree	$984,038	$147,746
Table total	$606,208	$108,168

Source: Primary data collected by Thomas D. Boston from City of Atlanta and Fulton County Certification Records.

income and racial characteristics of the neighborhoods where these firms are located. These firms are most heavily concentrated in construction (26.3 percent), business services (24.4 percent), engineering and management services (14.4 percent), and wholesale services (11.6 percent). For each industry group, the table gives the median income of the zip code where the firms are located.

The data reveal that firms located in the highest income neighborhoods tend to be concentrated in the following industries: business services ($40,577), communications, ($38,644), other retail ($37,383), other transportation services ($36,996), engineering and management services ($36,935), and wholesale ($34,812). By contrast, firms in the lowest income neighborhoods tend to be concentrated in real estate ($24,959), light manufacturing ($26,705), other services ($27,597) and personal services ($29,163). The percent of the population that is black residing in these neighborhoods is provided in the last column of the table.[24]

The last column provides insight into the kinds of industries that

Table 1.8 Industry distribution of African-American business by
neighborhood characteristics, Atlanta metropolitan area, 1993

Standard Industrial Classification	Number of firms	% of total	Neighborhood income[a]	Black population[b]
Agriculture and mining	3	0.4%	$53,981	41.0%
Business services	176	24.4%	$40,577	46.0%
Communications	4	0.6%	$38,644	45.0%
Other retail	25	3.5%	$37,383	45.0%
Other transportation	6	0.8%	$36,996	38.0%
Engineering and management services	104	14.4%	$36,935	51.0%
Wholesale	84	11.6%	$34,812	57.0%
Construction	190	26.3%	$33,612	64.0%
Health services	12	1.7%	$33,148	69.0%
Finance and insurance	13	1.8%	$32,755	53.0%
Local transportation and trucking	15	2.1%	$31,763	59.0%
Personal services	6	0.8%	$29,163	83.0%
Other services	56	7.8%	$27,597	74.0%
Light manufacturing	20	2.8%	$26,705	67.0%
Real estate	7	1.0%	$24,959	66.0%
Retail (food and eating)	1	0.1%	$19,333	75.0%
Total	722	100.0%	$35,291	57.0%

Source: Primary data collected by Thomas D. Boston from City of Atlanta and Fulton County
Certification Records.
Notes
[a] This value is derived for each industry by taking the average of the median income of zip
codes where firms are located.
[b] This value is derived for each industry by taking the average of the percent of blacks in
each zip code where firms are located.

tend to be located in neighborhoods of particular racial composition. For example, personal services are concentrated in
neighborhoods that are 83 percent black. Other industries found in
predominately black neighborhoods are: other services (74 percent),
health services (69 percent), light manufacturing (67 percent), real
estate (66 percent), and construction (64 percent).

Finally, Table 1.9 indicates how black-owned businesses are
distributed across neighborhoods according to the income of the
neighborhood and the revenue and employment characteristics of
the businesses. In poverty neighborhoods, that is neighborhoods
where the median family income is $15,000 or less, we find 3
percent of these black-owned businesses. Such neighborhoods
account for 14 percent of all families in the three-county Atlanta
Metropolitan Statistical Area (MSA), or 58,425 out of 417,618
families. In zip codes where the median family income is between
$15,000 and $25,000, we find 23.7 percent of all black-owned
businesses and 15.4 percent of all families, or 98,488 families.[25] In

Table 1.9 Distribution of African-American businesses by income characteristics of zip codes where they are located

Income class of zip code[a]	No. of firms	% of total	Mean revenue[b]	Median revenue[b]	Total employment in zip code	Mean employment per firm	Total black employment	Black employment as % of total employment
$0–4,999	20	2.9%	$2,089,239	$412,283	187	11.69	153	81.8%
$15,000–24,999	161	23.7%	$707,021	$140,151	1,724	11.34	1,323	76.7%
$25,000–39,999	255	37.5%	$263,719	$110,148	1,568	6.56	1,277	73.1%
$40,000–59,999	182	26.8%	$723,485	$53,357	1,267	7.28	926	74.6%
$60,000+	62	9.1%	$576,181	$145,289	476	8.07	355	77.1%
	680	100.0%	$606,268	$108,168	6,410	9.45	4,944	77.0%

Source: Primary data collected by Thomas D. Boston from City of Atlanta and Fulton County Certification Records.

Notes

[a] Based on 1990 Census.

[b] Of business in income class.

total, 26.6 percent of all black-owned businesses registered in these programs are located in neighborhoods where the median family income is $25,000 or less.

The most successful black-owned businesses as measured by average and median revenues are located in the lowest income neighborhoods. That is, the average revenue of businesses in neighborhoods where income is $15,000 or less is $2,089,239. Similarly, the median revenue of these firms is also higher than that of firms in other neighborhoods. Businesses in neighborhoods where family income varies between $15,000 and $25,000 recorded the second largest average revenues.

The 722 black-owned firms employ 9.5 workers on average. But firms in the lowest income neighborhoods employ over 11 workers on average. The second-to-last column of the table reports the percent of black employment within firms by income characteristics of neighborhoods. It reveals that 82 percent of the employees in black-owned firms in the lowest income neighborhood are black, while 75 percent of the employees in firms located in the highest income neighborhoods are black. In short, there is not much variation in racial employment patterns, regardless of where the firm is located.

There is a common perception that more successful black entrepreneurs are locating in the suburbs or in middle-income neighborhoods. But we have seen that some of the most successful firms participating in the minority business program of Atlanta tend to locate in lower income neighborhoods. Hence, minority business programs not only assist black business development, they also provide important economic benefits such as jobs and income to the segment of the community most in need.

The Atlanta experience demonstrates that affirmative action programs are not just vehicles for remedying past and present inequities; they are important contributors to income and employment opportunities in distressed urban areas.

2

STRICT SCRUTINY IS "STRICT IN THEORY AND FATAL IN FACT"

The Croson Decision

Historically, Congress has been endowed with unique powers to remedy past injustices and advance the social interest, even when such laws burden particular classes. From a legal standpoint, the remedies instituted by Congress to correct past racial injustices have been subject to a lesser standard of scrutiny by the Courts.

In the mid-1970s, Congress enacted laws requiring federal departments and agencies to take affirmative measures to correct the gross under-utilization of minorities and women in federal contracting. In 1977, the Public Works Employment Act mandated that, absent an administrative waiver, at least 10 percent of federal funds for local public works projects must be used by state and local grantees to procure services or supplies from minority businesses. Soon after the Act was established, H. Earl Fullilove and several associations of construction contractors challenged its constitutionality.[1] This was the first legal challenge to a federal set-aside program to reach the Supreme Court. In the petition, the constitutionality of the federal government's 10 percent set-aside provision, established by the Public Works Employment Act, was challenged. The suit alleged that Fullilove and others incurred injury due to the enforcement of the minority business requirement. They argued that the requirement violated the Equal Protection Clause of the Fourteenth Amendment and the Due Process Clause of the Fifth Amendment.

On 2 July 1980 the U.S. Supreme Court rendered a decision in the case. A plurality of Justices found the program to be constitutional. The decision allowed federal departments and agencies to operate minority business programs and state and local agencies felt that the ruling gave them the same latitude.

Cities felt a sense of security in pursuing affirmative action policies because federal agencies and departments were mandating that they do so as a prerequisite for receiving federal funds for local public works projects. Furthermore the Fullilove Decision appeared to codify the legality of these practices.

Justice Burger, writing a plurality opinion in Fullilove, concluded that Congress need not establish "specific findings of discrimination because it has broad authority and an affirmative duty to react to and address discrimination as a matter of national concern."[2] In drawing attention to the discriminatory record of the previous two decades, Justice Marshall argued that racial classifications are constitutional in remedying past discrimination if they serve important governmental interests and if they are substantially related to the achievement of those interests.[3] The test is whether there is a "rational relationship" between the remedy and the government's interest. Congress subsequently enacted affirmative action provisions in the Surface Transportation Assistance Act of 1982, the Foreign Assistance Act of 1983 and its 1985 extension, and the Surface Transportation and Uniform Relocation Assistance Act of 1987.

State and local agencies assumed they possessed similar powers as the federal government when it came to affirmative action policies. Thus, by 1988 there were programs at 190 local governmental agencies and at thirty-six state agencies

Strict scrutiny becomes the legal standard

The city of Richmond, Virginia, has a history that is tainted by the legacy of Jim Crow segregation. In recent times, Richmond attempted to dilute black voting rights (*Richmond* v. *United States*, 422 U.S. 358, 95 S. Ct. 2296, 45 L. Ed. 2d 245 (1975)), it resisted school desegregation and had a well established legacy of housing discrimination (*Bradley* v. *School Board of the City of Richmond*, 462 F.2d 1058, 1060, n.1 (CA4 1972)). The record of black business access to city procurement was equally terrible. Between 1978 and 1983, the city awarded only 0.67 percent of its prime construction contracts to minority firms.

Faced with this legacy of discrimination, in April of 1983 the city council voted to enact an affirmative action plan in contracting.[4] The purpose of the plan was to increase the participation of minority owned businesses in public construction contracts awarded by the city. In the course of the public hearings, evidence was introduced indicating that: (1) even though only 0.67 percent of the city's prime construction contracts went to minority firms over the previous five years, the city had a 50 percent black population; (2) the proposed ordinance was consistent with the Fullilove decision; (3) six local construction associations had virtually no minority members; and (4) widespread discrimination existed in the local, state and national construction industries.

The plan was enacted for a period of five years and included blacks, Hispanics, Asians, Eskimos and Aleuts. It required recipients of prime construction contracts to subcontract at least 30 percent of the contract's value to minority firms. A waiver from the goal was provided in cases where no suitable minority firms were available.

Five months after the enactment of the plan, the city invited bids for the installation of plumbing fixtures at the city jail. The J.A. Croson Company submitted the only bid on the project. Prior to doing so, the company contacted several minority businesses. One minority business contacted by Croson Company, Continental Metal Hose, expressed an interest in serving as a subcontractor on the project, but had to obtain a price quotation for fixtures before it could submit its bid. The supplier contacted by Continental had already submitted a bid to Croson and refused to provide a quote to Continental. Another supplier refused to provide Continental a quote until it had obtained a credit check, a procedure that would take a minimum of thirty days. Because of this, Croson submitted its bid without the minority requirement.

Shortly after the bid opening, Croson submitted a waiver requesting release from the minority requirement. Continental, learning of this, informed the city that it could supply the fixtures. However, its price was $6,183.29 higher than the price Croson had stipulated in its proposal. Croson was given ten days to comply with the minority requirement. Instead the company argued for a waiver or the right to increase the contract price. The city rejected both requests and decided to re-bid the contract. Croson filed suit in the district court claiming that the program was unconstitutional. The District Court upheld the constitutionality of the city's program. The U.S. Court of Appeals, using the Fullilove case as a standard, affirmed the district court's decision. Croson then appealed to the U.S. Supreme Court. The Court vacated the earlier decision and remanded the case back to the Fourth Circuit Court of Appeals in light of its decision in the Wygant case.[5] On remand, the Circuit Court reversed the district court's decision and ruled that the plan violated the equal protection clause of the Fourteenth Amendment because the city's plan did not conform to the strict scrutiny standard.

The Fourth Circuit Court's decision was appealed to the U.S. Supreme Court by the City of Richmond. This time the Supreme Court affirmed the Circuit Court's decision. It was the first time that a majority, rather than a plurality, agreed that strict scrutiny would be applied to racial preference programs.

The decision held that the program denied certain citizens the opportunity to compete for a fixed percentage of contracts based solely on their race. All classifications based on race, Justice Sandra Day O'Connor argued, whether benefiting or burdening minorities or non-minorities, will be subject to strict scrutiny. This means that the "factual predicate" underlying racial preference programs must be supported by adequate and specific findings of past discrimination. Generalized findings are not sufficient.

The majority opinion is divided into a number of parts. First, it affirms that strict scrutiny must be applied to all racial classifications whether benefiting or burdening minorities. On this issue Justice Marshall dissented. He argued that this standard should be applied to those classifications that discriminate against minorities but not those designed to eliminate past discrimination:

> In concluding that remedial classifications warrant no different standard of review under the Constitution than the most brute and repugnant forms of state-sponsored racism, a majority of this Court signals that it regards racial discrimination as largely a phenomenon of the past, and that government bodies need no longer preoccupy themselves with rectifying racial injustice. I, however, do not believe this Nation is anywhere close to eradicating racial discrimination or its vestiges. In constitutionalizing its wishful thinking, the majority today does a grave disservice not only to those victims of past and present racial discrimination in this Nation whom government has sought to assist, but also to this Court's long tradition of approaching issues of race with the utmost sensitivity.[6]

Second, the City of Richmond relied heavily upon the Fullilove Decision as a justification for its program. But in Croson, the majority ruled that sections 1 and 5 of the Fourteenth Amendment limit the powers of states, in contrast to the more sweeping powers of Congress. The latter was not required to meet the strict scrutiny standard, but states and localities are.

Third, the Court established a requirement that the factual predicate underlying the set-aside plan must be supported by adequate findings of past discrimination. A program cannot be justified on the argument that blacks constitute 50 percent of the local population but receive less than 1 percent of public contracts.

In establishing its program, the City of Richmond initially relied on statements of minority business owners attesting to their exclusion from the skilled trades and encounters with discrimination in the industry. Further, they argued that while minorities constituted 50 percent of the city's population, minority firms received less than one percent of prime contracts. But the Supreme Court ruled that their findings did not provide the city of Richmond with a strong basis of evidence to implement a remedial race-based program. Because the evidence presented did not point to specific discrimination, the Court ruled that the city had failed to demonstrate a compelling interest in establishing a race-based preference program.

Richmond was also criticized for including Spanish-speaking minorities, Orientals, Indians, Eskimos, and Aleuts in its plan when there was no evidence of past discrimination against them. Likewise, the Court was critical of the city's plan because it allowed all minorities to be eligible for the remedy no matter where they resided. Further the Court viewed the 30 percent minority requirement as a quota.

In the Croson decision, the majority ruled that a state or local entity might take action to rectify discrimination. "If the City of Richmond had evidence before it that non-minority contractors were systematically excluding minority businesses from subcontracting opportunities it could take action to end the discriminatory exclusion."[7] But the decision required that a disparity must be established between the utilization of minority contractors and their availability among all qualified, willing and able contractors in the market area. It noted that a pattern of individual discriminatory acts, if supported by appropriate statistical proof, is probative. Finally, it required local governments to establish a remedy that is consistent with the scope of the injury.

The decision also criticized the City of Richmond for not pursuing race-neutral devices such as simplifying bidding procedures, relaxing bonding requirements and providing technical assistance to minority bidders. Because the city had failed to take these issues into consideration, the plan was ruled unconstitutional.

The Croson decision left little doubt about how the Court would rule on state and local affirmative action programs not conforming to the strict scrutiny standard. The only question remaining was whether it would apply the same standard to programs of the federal government. Following Croson, strict scrutiny became the law of the land for state and local agencies.

Strict scrutiny reaches the federal government

Between January 1991 and June 1992, state and local governments spent more than $13 million on disparity studies, and the Urban Mass Transit Authority spent an additional $14 million.[8] In 1990, thirty-four disparity studies were commissioned to address the Croson standard. Their average cost was $243,913.[9]

Following Croson, federal agencies grew nervous about the direction of the Supreme Court. But they took comfort in knowing that the Court made a clear distinction between the unique powers of Congress to establish race-based remedies and the more limited powers of state and local governments. The stakes were high because in 1989 federal agencies and departments awarded $8.6 billion through such programs.

The distinction between the powers of federal, state and local agencies to implement racial mandates was dissolved in the June 1995 Supreme Court decision in the case of *Adarand Constructors* v. *Pena and the U.S. Department of Transportation*. The Supreme Court ruled in a five-to-four vote that strict scrutiny must be the standard of review for race-based programs of the federal government as well. In making this shift, the Court voided all previous rulings that interpreted the equal protection clause of the constitution as having a different application at different levels of government.

As recently as 1990, in the *Metro Broadcasting* v. *the Federal Communications Commission (FCC)* case, the Court upheld the constitutionality of an affirmative action plan to increase the number of broadcast licenses awarded to minorities. Diversity in broadcasting, the Court concluded, was felt to advance an important governmental interest. But Adarand invalidated the FCC ruling as well as the Fullilove decision.

In the Adarand Decision Justice Stevens sided with the minority, despite having sided with the majority in the Croson Decision. His reasoning was that federal affirmative action programs represent the will of our entire Nation's elected representatives, where local programs do not.

In the Adarand Decision the Supreme Court has established a new precedent for determining the legality of racial mandates at the federal level. But this is only part of the picture. In other rulings, the Court has also reversed earlier decisions concerning job bias, school desegregation and political redistricting. In May 1995, Governor Pete Wilson of California ordered an end to all state affirmative action programs not required by law or by a court decree. In June, the Board of Regents of California voted to end race and gender preferences in university system hiring and admissions. The State dropped all affirmative action employment policies in 1996 and all race-based admission formulas were discontinued in January of 1997.

In November 1996, Californians voted to approve Proposition 209, the so-called Civil Rights Initiative. It prohibits state and local governmental agencies from giving preferences to women and minorities in employment, promotions, contracts and college admissions. The Texas legislature implemented a similar policy in 1997, but the Houston electorate voted to maintain its minority business affirmative action plan.

The disparity study quagmire

Professor George La Noue and John Sullivan maintain a clearinghouse of disparity studies at the University of Maryland, Baltimore County. In 1996 their inventory consisted of 102 studies, conducted in twenty-seven different states and the District of Columbia. This is only a portion of the studies that have been commissioned. La Noue found that by the summer of 1994, state and local areas had spent more than $40 million on disparity studies.[10]

The cost of disparity studies is being driven by three factors. First, the Supreme Court Justices left numerous questions unanswered regarding the specific evidence required to meet strict scrutiny. As a result, consultants are afraid of the legal consequences of omitting something that may later prove to be important.

Second, the uncertainty over the appropriate evidence, along with the absence of a standard measure of cost, led to a situation whereby the very extensive Atlanta Disparity Study, completed in 1990 and supervised by economists Andrew Brimmer and Ray Marshall, set the initial methodology and market price. The Atlanta Study grew out of unique circumstances that were not present at other locations. Commissioned at over one-half-million dollars, this study covered contracting and procurement in the City of Atlanta and Fulton County. Following its commissioning in 1989, other public agencies gave in to a classic case of what economist Joseph Stiglitz has referred to as the dependence of quality on price. That is, due to the uncertainty concerning the standard of evidence, public agencies used the price of a disparity study as a signal of its quality. Agencies all over the country used Atlanta as a yardstick. In doing so, they reasoned that if they did not pay a hefty price, they were not getting a quality product.

By the time the Croson decision was rendered, the City of Atlanta had become the focal point for cities interested in implementing set-aside programs. Atlanta established a program in mid-1970. One decade later, most of the nation's programs were patterned after it. Andrew Young, Mayor of Atlanta, viewed the Croson decision as a challenge to the achievement of civil rights. As a result, the expense of complying with the decision's strict scrutiny standard was secondary in importance to the need to demonstrate nationally that the strict scrutiny standard could be met and that affirmative action is a legal remedy for past injustices.

Fueling the city's resolve was the fact that just three months after the Croson decision, the Georgia Supreme Court quoted Croson almost verbatim and struck down Atlanta's program.[11] The State Supreme Court argued that Atlanta, like Richmond, had failed to demonstrate a "compelling interest" and establish a "narrowly tailored program." At the same time that Atlanta's program was suspended, Fulton County's program was under legal attack.[12] So together these agencies decided to mount a major effort to meet the new Croson standard.

The team of consultants commissioned to undertake the Atlanta disparity study settled upon a basic methodology. This included a historical examination of the treatment of minorities in the Atlanta market, a statistical analysis of contracting and procurement, collection of anecdotal evidence of discrimination from 100 minority contractors, a study of discrimination in trade unions, an examination of woman business owners in the Atlanta market, and many other factors necessary to determine whether or not a disparity in minority utilization existed. If a disparity was proved to exist, the study sought to determine why. Numerous aspects of discriminatory treatment were examined. The end result was a disparity study containing eight volumes, over 1,069 pages, written by over a dozen different consultants.

Persistent legal challenges, even of very expensive studies, forced agencies to add more and more dollars to the disparity study coffers to attract the so-called best consultants to patch up perceived weaknesses in existing studies or conduct new studies. For example, nine agencies in the Memphis metropolitan area recently paid $1.3 million for a disparity study covering their contracting and procurement. Similarly, the cities of Miami and St. Louis spent hundreds of thousands of dollars on disparity studies and were forced to repeat these expenditures because the initial studies did not withstand court challenges.

Agencies are caught in a vicious circle. To rectify the effects of past discriminatory practices, they must pay large sums to comply with the Supreme Court mandate. But this mandate is somewhat vague on many issues related to the sufficiency of evidence. Further, the evidentiary standard is being redefined constantly.

In reality, the Croson requirement has become practically impossible to meet and as a result federal, state and local set-aside programs are being dismantled. The difficulty in meeting the standard resides in the fact that the kind of evidence required has not been clarified. It seems odd for the Supreme Court to impose the strict scrutiny standard in the Croson Decision and not take the opportunity in the subsequent Adarand Decision to clarify its specific evidentiary requirements.

It is understood that the burden of proof rests with the agency operating a race-conscious program. The question is what is acceptable proof? A few years ago George La Noue, the individual used most frequently as an expert witness by the opponents of affirmative action programs, suggested that disparity study consultants should use census data to meet the aspect of the strict scrutiny standard requiring a comparison between the share of minority firms available to receive awards and the share of awards they actually receive. Now he argues that census data are untenable, instead bid data should be used. Yet, it is widely known that many interested, qualified and able minority firms have registered with public agencies but never receive bid information nor are they solicited for informal price quotations by telephone. Therefore, they would not be included in bid data. So why should bid data be superior? Yes, bid data resolves some problems but it introduces others. La Noue also argues that using regression analyses "permits the examination of variables other than race or gender to see which explains the observed statistical disparities."[13] But econometricians learned decades ago that there are stochastic problems involved in using regression analyses in discrimination research.[14]

La Noue trumpets the use of bid data and regression analyses and many other procedures. It is not that his suggestions are without merit. The problem is, if consultants follow La Noue's recommendations literally, disparity studies would be even more costly to conduct and it is doubtful that they would be any more defensible against individuals wishing to find fault. Agencies cannot afford to commission disparity studies that would follow La Noue's suggestion to examine all competing explanations for the racial disparity in contracting.

Some competing explanations La Noue suggests as meriting examination are differences between minority-owned and majority-owned businesses and business owners in "size, geographical location, education, income, culture, English language fluency, and the timing and character of immigration of groups, etc."[15] At what point do we put the brakes on this type of inquiry and who will decide what competing explanations are worthy of investigation – Professor La Noue, or the Supreme Court that imposed the strict scrutiny requirement? Clearly this is a matter for the Court to decide.

If it is true that the Supreme Court intends for local agencies to examine every conceivable explanation for the differences in contracts awarded to minorities and non-minorities, then public agencies should save time and money by simply concluding that affirmative action programs are unconstitutional.

In theory, the law allows affirmative action programs to exist. In practice, however, they are becoming impossible. It is not that La Noue's line of inquiry is wrong, but why should it be superior to other approaches? Yet, the so-called "standard" he has advocated is being used to invalidate disparity studies and minority business programs across the country. What is needed instead of La Noue's standard is for the Court to establish an independent body such as a Judicial Commission, to set the guidelines for evidence and determine which methods are acceptable and, as a consequence, which are not.

It is worth noting Justice O'Connor's surprise when she was confronted with the implications of the strict scrutiny argument she advanced in the Croson decision. On 5 December 1995, the Supreme Court listened to arguments presented by plaintiffs seeking to strike down majority black voting districts in Texas and North Carolina. Robinson O. Everett told the Court that the districts must be found unconstitutional under their own previously applied principle of "strict scrutiny."

"So you take the position that once strict scrutiny is applied, it's fatal in fact," Justice O'Connor said. Her reference, not articulated but unmistakable, was not only her voting rights opinions but also her majority opinion for the Court last June in a Federal affirmative action case, in which she wrote that "we wish to dispel the notion that strict scrutiny is strict in theory but fatal in fact."

Yes, Mr. Everett replied, it was his position that no race-conscious districting could survive the hurdle of strict scrutiny.

Justice O'Connor said, "I had thought we had indicated it is possible to survive strict scrutiny, but you're arguing for something else."

Mr. Everett replied, "I'm descending from the theoretical to the practical."[16]

For the last forty years, since the publication of Gary Becker's *Economics of Discrimination*, economists have tried to establish a conclusive statistical proof of earnings discrimination. Elaborate regression equations have been constructed that control for numerous variables. When this procedure is used, the racial differential that remains after earnings-related attributes are controlled is attributed to discrimination. Some authors have gone so far as to develop elaborate simultaneous equation models in an attempt to control for the influence of discrimination in earlier periods on earnings-related attributes such as education and experience in the current period. But some researchers still object that factors not included in the regression equation influence the size of the unexplained racial earnings differential. In fact, regression equations cannot directly establish discrimination. All they can do is make judgments that rule out factors included in the equation and assume that that discrimination is approximated by the residual effect. Some researchers have attempted to measure discrimination directly through the use of testers.[17] But the use of testers has also raised validity questions.

What this means is that social scientists have not yet found a method that is definitive. They accept the unexplained residual approach in regression analyses as an approximation of discrimination, but this can also be problematic because of its limitations. So why should the legal profession or governmental agencies accept Professor La Noue's interpretation of a social science research standard for disparity studies? La Noue is just one more social scientist among thousands of others. *He has not found a solution to resolving the difficulties and ambiguities of meeting the strict scrutiny standard. He has simply packaged an approach for discrediting disparity studies that seek to do so.*

The vagueness of the guidelines for meeting strict scrutiny and the burdensome cost of complying with the Croson Decision are major impediments to equal treatment. In addition, some consultants have routinely overcharged agencies that have been naive enough to believe that quality depends upon price. No matter how costly, virtually all studies have been subjected to legal challenges. As far back as March 1991, just two years after the Croson Decision, of slightly over 200 programs nationally, sixty-six had been challenged legally; thirty-three had been voluntarily terminated; and sixty-five were under re-evaluation. Strict scrutiny is indeed "strict in theory" and "fatal in fact."

Federal response to the affirmative action challenge

In October 1995, the U.S. Department of Defense canceled a key provision of its minority preference program. The "rule of two" minority set-aside provision was canceled in response to the June 1995 U.S. Supreme Court decision in the case of *Adarand* v. *Pena*.

In announcing the cancellation of its "rule of two" program, the Defense Department eliminated a provision that was previously used to set aside defense contracts exclusively for minority firms. This provision was applied whenever there are two or more qualified minority firms bidding and when their price is not more than 10 percent of the fair market price. The Defense Department estimates that this will decrease awards to minorities by about $1 billion. Today all affirmative action policies to assist minority firms are under review. Conceivably, all could suffer the same fate as the "rule of two" program.

The Defense Department's minority procurement program is the largest of all federal departments, accounting for 58 percent of the total of federal procurement from minority firms. The Department of Transportation has the next most significant program. In fiscal 1994, it awarded $2.8 billion in procurement, grants and contracts to minorities.

It is no accident that the Defense Department's minority business program was the first to be canceled and the Department of Transportation's was challenged in the Adarand case. These two departments have done the most to assist minority firms. At present, there are twenty-six federal agencies or departments with minority business affirmative action programs. These programs spent $14.3 billion on minority procurement in the 1994 financial year, and an additional $5 billion in grants, contracts and loans with minority businesses and institutions such as historically black colleges and universities.

When Republicans gained control of the House and the Senate in 1994, affirmative action became a central focus of the legislative agenda. Then Senate Majority Leader Bob Dole requested that the Congressional Research Service prepare a comprehensive list of federal statutes, regulations, programs, and Executive orders granting preferences to individuals on the basis of race, sex, national origin or ethnic background.[18]

In July 1995, Senator Phil Gramm introduced legislation to prohibit agencies funded by House bill (H.R. 831) from awarding federal contracts on the basis of race, color, national origin or gender. The amendment was rejected by a vote of thirty-six to sixty-one. But a substitute amendment offered by Senator Patty Murray was approved. The substitute amendment "bars the use of funds made available by the appropriations act for programs that result in the awarding of Federal contracts to unqualified persons, in reverse discrimination, or in quotas, or for programs inconsistent with the Supreme Court's decision in the Adarand case."[19]

In the House, Gary Franks attempted to introduce an amendment to the Defense Appropriations Bill to ban federal contract set-asides for minorities and women but the House Rules Committee did not allow it. Also in July 1995, Senate Majority Leader Bob Dole and Representative Charles Canady, Chairman of the Constitution Subcommittee of the House Judiciary Committee, introduced companion bills (S. 1085, H.R. 2128), entitled the Equal Opportunity Act of 1995. The bills sought to bar the federal government from "intentionally discriminating against, or granting a preference to, any individual or group based on race, color, national origin, or seat in Federal contracting, Federal employment, or federally conducted programs. The bills would also prohibit the Government from requiring or encouraging Federal contractors to grant such preferences. Preferences are defined to include quotas, set-asides, numerical goals, timetables, and other numerical objectives."[20]

In March 1998, the Senate revisited this issue. Senator Mitch McConnell, a Kentucky Republican, introduced an amendment to a bill reauthorizing transportation projects over the next six years that would kill the Disadvantaged Business Enterprise Program that seeks to award 10 percent of highway construction contracts to minorities and women. Surprisingly, fifteen Republicans joined nearly all Democrats in a fifty-eight to thirty-seven vote against the amendment. The vote coincides with recent public opinion polls showing that people do not like quotas, but they support the goals of affirmative action.

In February 1995, President Clinton ordered a review of all federal affirmative action programs. In a 19 July 1995 address to the nation, he concluded that "affirmative action remains a useful tool for widening economic and educational opportunity.... When affirmative action is done right, it is flexible, it is fair, and it works."[21] His position is that we should "mend it, not end it."

Federal agencies were ordered by Clinton to comply with the Adarand Decision in the application of affirmative action: (1) no quotas in theory or practice; (2) no illegal discrimination of any kind, including reverse discrimination; (3) no preference for people who are not qualified for any job or other opportunity; and (4) as soon as a program has succeeded, it must be retired.

Despite the growing legal assaults on affirmative action, less than one in four Americans believe affirmative action programs should be eliminated. Most believe that, with adequate reforms, the added opportunities they create for minorities and women are good.[22] In fact, 60 percent of whites, 67 percent of blacks and 56 percent of men say affirmative action programs are good.

Conclusion

Unless the evidence required to meet strict scrutiny is specified in more detail, the end of affirmative action at the federal, state and local levels may occur. This will have dire consequences for many black-owned businesses. Black entrepreneurs still do not enjoy equal access to business opportunities in the private sector. If they must now face similar barriers in the public sector, their market share will shrink significantly. Public-sector procurement opportunities have provided black firms with an avenue to grow and diversify, but strict scrutiny is foreclosing this pathway.

In a dissenting opinion to the Croson decision, Justice Marshall stated:

> More fundamentally, today's decision marks a deliberate and giant step backward in this Court's affirmative action

jurisprudence. Cynical of one municipality's attempt to redress the effects of past racial discrimination in a particular industry, the majority launches a grapeshot attack on race-conscious remedies in general. The majority's unnecessary pronouncement will inevitably discourage or prevent governmental entities, particularly States and localities, from acting to rectify the scourge of past discrimination. This is the harsh reality of the majority's decision, but it is not the Constitution's command.[23]

By requiring local programs to meet the strict scrutiny standard, the Supreme Court has imposed an enormous burden on federal, state and local governmental agencies. The fact-finding methodology needed to establish the burden of proof is unclear. While this requirement seems reasonable in theory, in practice it is a hurdle that has become almost impossible to overcome. Furthermore, the financial burden of assembling the required proof is daunting.

Neither the Croson Decision nor the Adarand Decision resolve the specific kind of evidence needed to establish the burden of proof; they only provide broad guidelines. This ambiguity has led consultants to take a shotgun approach to collecting information for disparity studies, an approach that is very expensive. More extensive investigations are always assumed to be better – despite the cost. Yet, volumes of research cannot insulate agencies from the persistent legal challenges by organizations like the Associated General Contractors. In fact, the mere threat of a legal challenge has killed many minority business programs – even after hundreds of thousands of dollars have been spent on disparity studies. These same threats have prompted other agencies to indefinitely postpone implementing the recommendations of disparity studies. Many others now believe it is futile to even commission a study.

Millions of dollars have been paid to consultants for these studies. But the lack of objective-detailed directions from the Supreme Court and inconsistent findings among lower courts has made disparity studies expensive and usually indefensible in the face of a legal challenge.

Given the broad guidelines provided by the Supreme Court and the varying interpretations of lower courts, strict scrutiny has become a bed of quicksand for affirmative action programs. Supreme Court Justices Thomas and Scalia favor the dismantling of all programs involving racial mandates. Several well-known opposition groups share this view and have engaged in or supported legal challenges to these programs.

Affirmative action programs are being dismantled not because discrimination has ceased to exist, but because of the ambiguous guidelines required to document it. In the process, minorities are being denied compensation for decades of racial exclusion from public-sector procurement.

If the guarantees of the Fifth and Fourteenth Amendments are to remain available to historically disadvantaged minorities, independent and objective parties must establish a clear standard of evidence. Partisan opponents of affirmative action should not establish the standard. Today, almost every race-conscious program is the target of legal challenges no matter how well documented its factual predicate is. Local agencies are caught in a "no win" situation as they seek to guarantee the rights of minority businesspersons historically excluded from procurement opportunities. The strategy of organizations and individuals hostile to affirmative action is to persuade the courts to demand great specificity in the evidence of discrimination. The specificity of evidence and ambiguity of method are very costly to local and state governments, and represent quicksand for affirmative action programs.

Some of the evidence demanded by opponents of affirmative action is legitimate, but even when disparity studies conform, programs are still sued and studies are branded as "fatally flawed." The court must now give judicial guidance on the method for complying with strict scrutiny. If affirmative action programs fail under objective guidelines for strict scrutiny, then fine, they should not exist. But this is not the situation today. At present strict scrutiny is "strict in theory and fatal in fact." Therefore, a Judicial Commission on Strict Scrutiny is desperately needed.

3

RECENT TRENDS AMONG BLACK-OWNED BUSINESSES IN ATLANTA

Why all the fuss about Atlanta?

Black-owned businesses comprise one of the City of Atlanta's most important resources. According to a survey conducted by the author in 1995, these businesses currently generate 7,430 jobs in the city (which is 5.9 percent of the City's workforce) and about 15,000 jobs in the metropolitan area. At their current growth rate, these businesses will employ 24,289 City workers by the year 2010. This employment capacity could accommodate 15 percent of the city's 2010 black workforce, estimated to be 162,196.[1] If future conditions simulate present conditions, 82 percent of the jobs created by black-owned businesses will go to blacks.

The growth rate of black-owned businesses in the metropolitan area is almost twice that of businesses located in the city. But even if the current metro rate tapers from 14.7 percent to 10 percent, by the year 2010 there should be about 130,000 black-owned businesses employing close to 60,000 workers.[2] This indicates that increasing the number of black-owned businesses can be an effective strategy for reducing the racial disparity in unemployment.

In 1995, the author mailed a survey to 1,412 minority and women-owned businesses located in the Atlanta metropolitan area. Three hundred and sixteen firms responded, including 224 black-owned businesses. The results, which are discussed in detail later in this chapter, indicate that a new black entrepreneur has emerged. These new entrepreneurs are typically well educated, young, have managerial and executive experience, and operate in more diversified fast-growing industries. Their businesses and professional backgrounds are very different from the old "black bourgeoisie" that E. Franklin Frazier criticized for being "mom and pop" proprietors.[3] Three decades ago most successful black entrepreneurs served a black clientele and were concentrated in personal service or retail industries. But this has changed, as Jeanne Saddler of the *Wall Street Journal* recently observed. Black business owners are undergoing a transformation. They are beginning to push the business envelope. "Ambitious young black professionals," Saddler notes, "are starting new businesses at a rapid clip, often at very early ages. They have more financial wherewithal than their predecessors, are bigger risk takers and, while creating jobs for minorities, often set up shop in mostly white business districts rather than poor inner-city neighborhoods."[4]

You will see that the survey results dispel the popular notion that successful black-owned businesses have moved to the suburbs and no longer hire blacks and inner city residents. City residents are still employed by black-owned businesses located in the suburbs. Although the growth in the number of black-owned businesses located in the suburbs is faster than growth in the city, the employment opportunities accruing for city residents as a result of suburban growth is an important by-product of the city's policies of providing equal business opportunity.

For example, the survey results indicate that 82 percent of the employees in black-owned businesses located within the City of Atlanta are black. Additionally, 25 percent reside in low-income inner city neighborhoods and 59 percent are city residents. Among black-owned businesses located in the Atlanta suburbs, 85 percent of their employees are black, 19 percent come from low-income inner city communities and 36 percent reside in the City of Atlanta.

The changes that are taking place among black-owned businesses are not always visible because the new businesses are not storefront establishments. A second reason these changes are not readily apparent is because the government census survey that most researchers rely on for five-year updates on the number and size of black-owned businesses, does not include information on all black-owned businesses.

In the 1987 and 1992 *Survey of Minority-Owned Business Enterprises: Black* (SMOBE)[5] the Census Bureau did not include information on the 1120 subchapter C corporations, but only on the 1120 S corporations. By including corporations only if they are 1120 subchapter S corporations and omitting 1120 subchapter C corporations from its survey universe, census data understates total employment in black-owned firms by at least 27 percent, and financial capacity by 23 percent.[6] Other research indicates that employment and revenue are understated by as much as 50 percent or more.[7] According to the 1992 SMOBE, black-owned S corporations comprised just 4 percent of all black-owned businesses but accounted for 38 percent of all business revenue and 51 percent of all employees in black-owned firms. Black-owned C corporations, those omitted from the census, have an even larger average employment and revenue capacity. The last year that the Census Bureau included both 1120 S and C corporations in its survey was 1982. Afterwards, it dropped C corporations because of the cost and difficulty involved in identifying the ethnicity of shareholders. For 1982, results are tabulated both ways. In 1982, total employment in black-owned firms including C corporations amounted to 165,765. By eliminating C corporations from the survey, total employment is reduced to 121,373. The SMOBE limitation contributes to the perception that black-owned businesses still have very marginal employment and income capacities. While significant growth is taking place among C corporations, these businesses are not included in the SMOBE data.

The Census Bureau is aware of this omission[8] and has changed its survey methodology for the SMOBE conducted in 1997. But until the new survey is released, it is important to keep this limitation in mind when attempting to gauge the current employment and revenue potential of African-American businesses.[9]

Survey of black-owned businesses in Atlanta

In the spring of 1995, the author conducted a survey of black-owned businesses in the Atlanta metropolitan area. The survey was conducted with the cooperation of the following public and private agencies: The Atlanta Business League, the City of Atlanta Office of Contract Compliance, Atlanta Public Schools Office of Contract Compliance, Fulton County Office of Contract Compliance, Georgia Minority Supplier Development Council, Dekalb County Office of Contract Compliance, Grady Health Systems Disadvantaged Business Enterprise Program, and the Metropolitan Atlanta Rapid Transit Authority. Each organization provided its list of minority-owned businesses. The comprehensive list consisted of 1,412 unique minority and women-owned businesses that operate in the Atlanta metropolitan area.

These 1,412 businesses are engaged in the industries identified in Table 3.1. Specifically, the industry breakdown is provided in the columns labeled "population." The word population in this survey is used in the statistical sense and refers to the original 1,412 businesses. The industries these businesses operate in are as follows: 40 percent are in services, 24 percent construction, 14 percent wholesale, 7 percent manufacturing, 5 percent transportation and communications, 4 percent retail, 2 percent finance, insurance and real estate, and 2 percent non-classified industries. Among the firms in service industries, the largest concentrations are computer and data processing followed by engineering and architectural services, services to buildings, management and public relation, commercial printing, personnel supply services, other business services, and advertising.

The survey response rate (excluding bad addresses) was 28 percent or 316. Weights were applied to the responses to make the industry distribution of the survey respondents identical to the industry distribution of the business population from which the survey is drawn (see Appendix for the weights and the adjusted survey distribution for black businesses when these weights are applied). An unweighted total of 224 black-owned firms responded to the survey. These represent a weighted total of 1,006 firms.

Table 3.2 indicates that 71 percent of the businesses responding to the survey are black-owned, while 14 percent are owned by white women, 7 percent by Hispanics, 5 percent by Asian and Pacific Islanders and 1 percent by Native Americans. In Table 3.3, the industry distribution of firms in the survey is reorganized into categories that correspond to the industry categories of the Census Bureau's SMOBE for the Atlanta metropolitan area. The primary difference between the two distributions is that black-owned firms

Table 3.1 Industry distribution of minority and women-owned businesses registered with various business assistance programs in the eighteen-county Atlanta metropolitan area, 1995

Industry	Population / (%)	Responses / (%)
Services	559 (40%)	153 (35%)
Construction	337 (24%)	52 (16%)
Wholesale	193 (14%)	37 (12%)
Manufacturing	96 (7%)	13 (4%)
Transportation, communications	67 (5%)	18 (6%)
Retail	62 (4%)	18 (6%)
Finance, insurance, real estate	28 (2%)	14 (4%)
Non-classified	70 (5%)	11 (3%)
Total	1,412 (100%)	316 (100%)

Source: Primary data compiled by Thomas D. Boston.

Table 3.2 Ethnic distribution of business owners responding to survey

Ethnicity of survey respondent	%
African-American	71%
White women	14%
Hispanic-American	7%
Asian/Pacific-American	5%
Native American/Eskimo	1%
Other/not identified	2%

Source: Survey conducted by Thomas D. Boston.

Table 3.3 Industry distribution of black-owned businesses in the Atlanta metropolitan area

Industry	Business survey population / (%)	SMOBE census population / (%)
Services	404 (40%)	12,640 (54%)
Construction	253 (25%)	1,865 (8%)
Wholesale	141 (14%)	570 (2%)
Manufacturing	66 (7%)	289 (1%)
Transportation, communications	30 (3%)	1,739 (7%)
Retail	41 (4%)	2,974 (13%)
Finance, insurance, real estate	20 (2%)	1,851 (8%)
Non-classified	51 (5%)	1,559 (7%)
Total	1,006 (100%)	23,487 (100%)

Source: SMOBE and survey data. SMOBE Census data is derived from the U.S. Dept. of Commerce, Bureau of the Census, *Survey of Minority-owned Business Enterprises: Black*, 1992 Economic Census, MBq2–1, p.19. Survey data are primary data compiled by Thomas D. Boston.

in the sample are more concentrated in construction, wholesale, and manufacturing, and less concentrated in services (particularly personal services), retail, transportation, and communications.

The geographic location of these firms is an issue that is vitally important to policy makers. The survey results reveal that 42.5 percent are within the city limits of Atlanta while 57.5 percent are located in suburbs, which are bounded by the eighteen-county metro area. Different factors motivate the decision to locate in the city as opposed to the suburbs.

The main reasons why black business owners located their businesses in the city are listed in the first column of Table 3.4. Among businesses located in the city, 25.4 percent give cost considerations as the most important factor while 14.7 percent give as their major reason the need to be close to their customers and clients. Additionally, 12.8 percent indicate that the convenience and accessibility is most important while 12.6 percent say that they did so to be close to home. Among businesses located in non-city locations of the metro area, 25.7 percent indicate they did so to be close to their customers and clients, 16.8 percent indicated that their major reason is the convenience and accessibility, 14.1 percent indicated cost considerations, and 9.8 percent indicated that it is because they have a home office. So cost is the driving factor behind black-owned businesses choosing to locate in the city while proximity to customers and clients is the primary determinant for black-owned businesses choosing to locate in the suburbs. In the survey, this was an open-ended question and the responses were all coded into common categories.

Table 3.4 Factors affecting black-owned business location decisions in metropolitan Atlanta

	Atlanta city limits (% distribution)	Other metro locations (% distribution)	Table total (% distribution)
Cost effective	25.4%	14.1%	20.5%
Close to customers/clients	14.7%	25.7%	19.5%
Convenient and accessible	12.8%	16.8%	14.6%
Close to home	12.6%	8.5%	10.8%
Home office	12.0%	9.2%	10.8%
Close to CBD	1.2%	11.6%	5.7%
Close to the Interstate	5.9%	1.4%	3.9%
For employee's convenience	3.3%	1.2%	2.4%
Market demographics	0.7%	2.7%	1.5%
Transit accessible	2.6%	–	1.5%
Prestige and visibility	0.7%	2.4%	1.4%
Acquired existing business	2.2%	–	1.2%
Unique facilities	1.1%	1.2%	1.1%
Close to airport	2.0%	–	1.1%
Close to suppliers	1.9%	–	1.1%
Political correctness	0.9%	0.9%	0.9%
Availability of parking	–	1.6%	0.7%
Other	–	1.6%	0.7%
Own the property	–	1.0%	0.4%
To avoid competitors	0.1%	–	0.1%
Total	100%	100%	100%

Source: 1995 survey conducted by Thomas D. Boston.

When businesses choose to locate in the suburbs, the decision also means that they are much less accessible by public transportation modes. For example, 98.2 percent of the black-owned businesses in the city are within walking distance to public transportation, while only 62.9 percent of black-owned businesses in the suburbs are. Nevertheless, it is still worth noting that over one-third of the employees in black-owned businesses located in the suburbs are city residents while only 59.3 percent of the employees in city businesses are city residents.

These survey results do not support the prevailing notion that black-owned businesses in the suburbs do not provide employment opportunities for city residents, low income city residents or for blacks in general (see Table 3.5, Table 3.6 and Table 3.7). Until now, most opinions on this issue have been formed by anecdotes, but Table 3.5 reveals that among businesses located within the city, 59 percent of their workers also reside in the city. Among non-city businesses, 35.8 percent of employees reside in the city. In general, 45.7 percent of all workers employed in black-owned businesses reside in the city, 16.4 percent live outside of the city but within the perimeter (the Interstate 285 highway that encircles the city), and 34.5 percent reside outside of the perimeter but within the five-county metro area.

It is also interesting to note that successful city and suburban black-owned businesses hire from low-income inner city neighborhoods. Data reveals that black-owned businesses hire 21.5 percent of their workforce from low-income inner-city neighborhoods. In

Table 3.5 Place of residence of majority of workers at metropolitan Atlanta black-owned businesses

	Atlanta city limits (% distribution)	Other metro locations (% distribution)	Table total (% distribution)
Close to CBD	32.1%	22.1%	26.3%
Outside of CBD but within city	27.2%	13.7%	19.4%
Outside city, within perimeter	19.7%	14.0%	16.4%
Outside perimeter (within MSA)	18.2%	46.6%	34.5%
Outside five-county MSA	1.7%	1.3%	1.5%
Missing values	1.1%	2.3%	1.8%
Total	100%	100%	100%

Source: 1995 survey conducted by Thomas D. Boston.

Table 3.6 Employees residing in low-income inner-city neighborhoods for metropolitan Atlanta black-owned businesses (mean %)

	Atlanta city limits	Other metro locations	Table total
Business services	14.5%	19.4%	17.3%
Construction	27.2%	27.5%	27.4%
Wholesale	21.8%	11.3%	15.0%
Manufacturing	51.3%	18.8%	33.2%
Transportation, communications	30.7%	15.3%	21.9%
Retail	31.7%	15.6%	21.4%
Finance, insurance, real estate	2.2%	0.0%	1.6%
Consumer services	38.3%	26.1%	30.7%
Non-classified	45.4%	0.0%	28.4%
Table mean	24.6%	19.2%	21.5%

Source: 1995 survey conducted by Thomas D. Boston.

Table 3.7 African-American employees in metropolitan Atlanta black-owned businesses (mean %)

	Atlanta city limits	Other metro locations	Table total
Construction	80.7%	81.3%	81.1%
Manufacturing	81.7%	74.0%	76.9%
Transportation, communications	86.7%	94.0%	91.3%
Wholesale	77.4%	88.4%	84.5%
Finance, insurance, real estate	95.0%	66.5%	88.7%
Retail	95.8%	81.6%	86.4%
Consumer services	83.0%	85.2%	84.3%
Business services	80.6%	86.8%	84.1%
Non-classified	84.0%	98.0%	89.3%
Table mean	81.8%	84.9%	83.6%

Source: 1995 survey conducted by Thomas D. Boston.

general, city businesses employ a larger percentage of their workforce from low-income inner-city neighborhoods than do non-city businesses. Table 3.6 indicates that 24.6 percent of employees in businesses located in the city live in low-income inner-city neighborhoods. Similarly, 19.2 percent of employees in non-city businesses are from low-income neighborhoods.

Table 3.7 shows that 83.6 percent of employees in black-owned firms are black. Among businesses located in the city, 81.8 percent of their employees are black, while 84.9 percent of employees are black in businesses located in non-city areas. Businesses in non-city areas still tend to locate in predominately black neighborhoods, and their location pattern in the suburbs have generally followed the distribution of the black population. For example, the average proportion of blacks in neighborhoods where black businesses in the city are located is 63.9 percent, while in Fulton County outside of Atlanta it is 75 percent, in suburban Cobb and Dekalb Counties it is 45.7 percent. These three counties have large black suburban populations. Again, this pattern indicates that black-owned businesses in the suburbs tend to locate in neighborhoods where the representation of blacks is significant. This also partially explains the predominately black employment pattern of black-owned suburban firms.

Black-owned businesses included in our survey are very dependent upon government contracting. For example, businesses located in the city of Atlanta derive 39.8 percent of their annual revenue in the government sector. The comparable figure for black businesses in the metro area is 32.4 percent (see Table 3.8). The results reveal that firms in the construction industry are very dependent on government sector revenue, with 55.2 percent derived in this sector, while firms in the transportation and communications industry are least dependent.

Table 3.9 shows how black business owners in Atlanta feel about affirmative action programs; 87.9 percent of owners with businesses located within the city limits and 87 percent of owners with suburban business locations strongly agree or agree that these programs are beneficial to the development of black-owned businesses.

Until recently, minority business programs existed at every major public agency in the City of Atlanta, but in the spring of 1997, programs at the Atlanta School System and the Atlanta-Fulton Hospital Authority were suspended as a result of legal challenges.

Personal characteristics of Atlanta's black business owners

An analysis of the gender of respondents indicates that men own 77.8 percent of the black-owned firms. Women are more heavily concentrated in business services (43 percent women versus 37 percent men), wholesale (21 percent women versus 12 percent men) and retail (6 percent women versus 3 percent men). By contrast, men dominate the construction trade (30 percent men versus 9

Table 3.8 Revenue from government sector for metropolitan Atlanta black-owned businesses (mean %)

	Atlanta city limits	Other metro locations	Table total
Business services	41.3%	23.5%	31.5%
Construction	55.2%	54.1%	54.5%
Wholesale	37.1%	27.9%	30.6%
Manufacturing	25.0%	7.1%	15.1%
Transportation, communications	5.0%	17.7%	13.5%
Retail	31.7%	31.3%	31.4%
Finance, insurance, real estate	27.7%	2.5%	22.1%
Consumer services	31.0%	37.8%	35.0%
Non-classified	22.0%	37.0%	27.6%
Table mean	39.8%	32.4%	35.4%

Source: 1995 survey conducted by Thomas D. Boston.

Table 3.9 Survey question: "Minority business affirmative action programs are important vehicles for aiding black business development"

	Atlanta city limits(% of total)	Other metro locations (% of total)	Table total (% of total)
Strongly agree	64.7%	63.8%	64.2%
Agree	23.2%	23.2%	23.2%
Neither agree nor disagree	5.9%	8.5%	7.4%
Disagree	0.6%	2.5%	1.7%
Strongly disagree	3.5%	0.8%	2.0%
Missing value	2.1%	1.1%	1.5%
Total	100%	100%	100%

Source: 1995 survey conducted by Thomas D. Boston.

percent women). On average, these firms have been in operation for 11.4 years; 12.4 years for firms located in the city limits and 10.7 years for suburban firms. Further, one-half of these owners (50.4 percent) are less than 44 years of age and 84.6 percent are 54 years of age or younger. As mentioned earlier, these business owners are young, well educated and operate in non-traditional industries.

Table 3.10 gives the educational attainment of black business owners by gender. The owners of businesses located in the city have a much higher educational attainment than do suburban owners. For example, 74.8 percent of owners with businesses located in the city have a college degree or better, as compared to 61.5 percent of owners in non-city locations; furthermore, the attainment among women is higher than it is among men. Among black women, 83 percent have completed college or better while among black men across all locations in the metro area, only 62.5 percent have completed college or better. *The Characteristics of Business Owners*, published by the Census Bureau, indicates that among the nation's non-minority male business owners, only 35.1 percent have a college education or better.[10]

Table 3.10 Educational attainment (by gender) of metropolitan Atlanta black business owners

	Atlanta city limits (% distribution)	Other metro locations (% distribution)	Table total (% distribution)
Male			
Some H.S., no degree	2.2%	2.5%	2.4%
H.S. degree	6.4%	6.6%	6.5%
Technical, vocational degree	2.0%	12.6%	8.0%
Some college, assoc. degree	15.8%	22.2%	19.4%
College graduate	29.1%	18.6%	23.1%
Some graduate school	8.8%	13.1%	11.2%
Graduate of professional degree	34.7%	23.2%	28.2%
Missing values	1.0%	1.2%	1.1%
Female			
Some H.S., no degree	–	–	–
H.S. degree	–	–	–
Technical, vocational degree	–	0.4%	0.2%
Some college, assoc. degree	16.9%	16.5%	16.7%
College graduate	30.4%	42.6%	37.7%
Some graduate school	29.4%	15.0%	20.8%
Graduate of professional degree	23.2%	25.5%	24.6%
Missing values	0.1%	–	–
Table total			
Some H.S., no degree	1.8%	2.0%	1.9%
H.S. degree	5.0%	5.1%	5.1%
Technical, vocational degree	1.6%	9.7%	6.3%
Some college, assoc. degree	16.0%	20.9%	18.8%
College graduate	29.4%	24.2%	26.4%
Some graduate school	13.1%	13.6%	13.3%
Graduate of professional degree	32.3%	23.7%	27.4%
Missing values	0.8%	0.9%	0.9%
Total	100%	100%	100%

Source: 1995 survey conducted by Thomas D. Boston.

Table 3.11 Previous work experience (by gender) for black business owners in metropolitan Atlanta

	Atlanta city limits (% distribution)	Other metro locations (% distribution)	Table total (% distribution)
Male			
Managerial/executive	44.9%	41.0%	42.7%
White collar (supervisor)	10.9%	14.8%	13.1%
White collar (non-super)	19.1%	14.0%	16.2%
Blue collar (supervisor)	8.4%	12.1%	10.5%
Blue collar (non-super)	5.1%	11.0%	8.4%
Unemployed	–	3.4%	1.9%
Homemaker	–	–	–
Other	11.5%	2.4%	6.4%
Missing values	–	1.5%	0.8%
Total	100%	100%	100%
Female			
Managerial/executive	55.7%	33.4%	42.3%
White collar (supervisor)	11.5%	16.8%	14.7%
White collar (non-super)	16.4%	36.9%	28.7%
Blue collar (supervisor)	–	2.6%	1.5%
Blue collar (non-super)	5.5%	6.5%	6.1%
Unemployed	–	–	–
Homemaker	–	2.8%	1.7%
Other	5.5%	1.1%	2.8%
Missing Values	5.5%	–	2.2%
Total	100%	100%	100%
Table total			
Managerial/executive	47.2%	39.2%	42.6%
White collar (supervisor)	11.0%	15.2%	13.5%
White collar (non-super)	18.6%	19.3%	19.0%
Blue collar (supervisor)	6.7%	9.9%	8.5%
Blue collar (non-super)	5.2%	9.9%	7.9%
Unemployed	–	2.6%	1.5%
Homemaker	–	0.6%	0.4%
Other	10.3%	2.1%	5.6%
Missing values	1.1%	1.1%	1.1%
Total	100%	100%	100%

Source: 1995 survey conducted by Thomas D. Boston.

These data reveal that 77.3 percent of black business owners are first-generation owners while 16.6 percent are second-generation owners, and the overwhelming majority of business owners were managers and executives prior to becoming entrepreneurs (see Table 3.11). The table indicates that 42.6 percent were former managers and executives. While this percent is not much different for men and women, it does vary by gender in city and non-city locations: 55.7 percent of black women owning businesses in the city were former managers and executives as compared to only 33.4 percent for black women with businesses located in the suburbs.

An examination of the legal form of ownership of these businesses indicates that 20.4 percent are proprietorships, 2.1 percent are partnerships, 27.1 percent are 1120 S corporations, 48.4 percent are 1120 C corporations and 2 percent are franchises. The fact that two-thirds of black corporations are C corporations reinforces the point made earlier about the limitation of SMOBE data. In particular, the Census survey does not include information on C corporations and as such its picture of the financial and employment capacity of black-owned businesses is limited. The average employment of businesses in the survey is 15.9 employees. Total employment in all firms surveyed is 15,127; in S corporations it is 5,722 while in C corporations it is 7,643. If we do not include C corporations, as SMOBE does not, the report would capture only 50 percent of the total employment capacity of the black-owned firms in this survey.

Whether their businesses are located in the city or in the suburbs, black business owners express a strong loyalty to the black community and feel they have a special responsibility towards revitalizing it. For example, 83.4 percent of business owners located in the city feel a special sense of responsibility to improving black communities, while 81.3 percent of suburban owners feel this way. Finally, only 36.1 percent of black business revenue is generated with blacks (see Table 3.12). This is a significant change from the days when blacks constituted the main clientele of black-owned firms because personal service and retail establishments constituted their main types of establishments. The survey results of this chapter reinforce one of the main themes of the book. A new generation of black-owned businesses has emerged in response to new opportunities made available to black business owners.

Table 3.12 African-American customers/clients at metropolitan Atlanta black-owned businesses (mean %)

	Atlanta city limits	Other metro locations	Table total
Business services	29.3%	37.5%	33.8%
Construction	42.5%	30.7%	34.8%
Wholesale	32.1%	37.4%	35.7%
Manufacturing	60.5%	14.2%	34.8%
Transportation, communications	17.0%	42.8%	31.7%
Retail	70.0%	23.9%	40.6%
Finance, insurance, real estate	67.9%	45.0%	62.8%
Consumer services	60.7%	34.6%	44.9%
Non-classified	48.0%	50.7%	49.0%
Table mean	38.9%	34.1%	36.1%

Source: 1995 survey conducted by Thomas D. Boston.

4

A SNAPSHOT OF THE PAST WHEN EQUAL BUSINESS OPPORTUNITY DID NOT EXIST

The historical record

The City of Atlanta was chartered in 1847 and the presence of successful black-owned businesses can be traced to the turn of the twentieth century. By 1890, the 28,098 blacks residing in the city constituted 43 percent of its population, but a rapid in-migration of whites occurred at the turn of the century. This caused the black population to decrease to 39 percent by 1900, 34 percent by 1910 and 31 percent by 1920. In 1930, the black population increased to 33 percent and remained at that level until 1960 when blacks constituted 38 percent of Atlanta's population. During the 1960s, whites moved to the suburbs in such great numbers that by 1970 the city's population of 495,000 residents was 51 percent black. Suburban movement of whites continued between 1980 and 1990, causing Atlanta's population to decrease to 394,000 while the metropolitan area gained 725,000 residents during the decade. The loss of white residents to the suburbs boosted the city's black presence to 67.1 percent of the total population.[1]

Even though blacks represented a large percentage of Atlanta's population and they had operated prosperous business ventures since the beginning of the twentieth century, 126 years passed before the city awarded a procurement contract to a black-owned firm. The award was for $13,000 in 1973.

It is virtually impossible to rationalize this racial exclusion. Not only were there qualified black entrepreneurs in Atlanta, but the historical record indicates that, prior to the passage of laws aimed at driving black contractors out of the local marketplace, blacks were as competitive in some areas as their white counterparts.

Prior to the Civil War, black free artisans and slaves served as contract laborers in urban and rural areas, and in many Southern cities they dominated the skilled trades. Grant's recent history documents this for Georgia:

> Many free Negroes were skilled workers, and some acted as independent contractors. Favored slaves were carpenters, blacksmiths, coopers, metalworkers, seamstresses, cooks, and teamsters. Some were able to parley these skills into small businesses after the Civil War; in fact, blacks dominated the skilled-artisan work at first. Since whites no longer had to compete with the unpaid labor of slaves, they gradually moved into these occupations. This increased competition helped lead the increasing Jim Crow that began in the 1880's. One goal was to force blacks from the more desirable jobs that were beginning to elevate some of them into the middle class's lower ranks.[2]

In 1818, the Georgia General Assembly made it unlawful for free blacks to immigrate into the state. By the 1830s, Southern legislatures passed laws prohibiting blacks from working in skilled trades. The Georgia Legislature was the leader among southern states in passing racially motivated laws.

In 1845 the Georgia Legislature passed an Act that legally prohibited blacks from making contracts. The law imposed a maximum penalty of $200 on whites for engaging in commerce with blacks. To appreciate the magnitude of a $200 penalty imposed in 1845, we compounded it at 4 percent annually for 151 years. The value of this fine today is $74,656. It must have been large enough to deter whites from trading with blacks. The legislation reads as follows:

> An act to prohibit colored mechanics and masons, being slaves or free persons of color, being mechanics or masons, from making contracts for the erection of buildings, or for the repair of buildings, and declaring the white person or persons directly or indirectly contracting with or employing them, as well as the master, employer, manager, or agent for said slave, or guardian for said free person of color, authorizing or permitting the same, guilty of a misdemeanor.

Section 1. Be it enacted by the Senate and the House of Representatives of the State of Georgia in General Assembly met, and it hereby enacted by the authority of the same, that from and after the first day of February next, each and every white person who shall hereafter contract or bargain with any slave mechanic, or mason, or free person of color, being a mechanic or mason, shall be liable to be indicted for a misdemeanor; and on conviction, to be fined, at the discretion of the court, not exceeding two hundred dollars.[3]

Charles Lyell's objection to the passage of this law reveals some hidden motives for it.

I may first observe in regard this disgraceful law, which is only carried by a small majority in the Georgian Legislature, that it proves that not a few of the Negro race having got so well in the world in reputation and fortune, and in skill in certain arts, that it was worth while to legislate against them in order to keep them down, and prevent them from entering into successful rivalry with whites. It confirms, therefore, most fully the impression which all I saw in Georgia had left on my mind, that the blacks are steadily rising in social importance in spite of slavery, or to speak more correctly, by aid of that institution.[4]

In 1858, 200 jealous white mechanics appealed to the Atlanta City Council to protect them from the market competition of black contractors.

We, the undersigned, would respectfully represent to your honorable body that there exists in the City of Atlanta a number of men who, in the opinion of your memorialist, are of no benefit to the city. We refer to Negro mechanics whose masters reside in other places, and who pay nothing toward the support of the city government, and whose Negro mechanics can afford to outbid the regular resident citizen mechanics of your city to their great injury, and without benefit to the city in any way. We most respectfully request your honorable body to take the matter in hand, and by your action on the premises afford such protection to the resident mechanics of your city as your honorable body may deem.[5]

During the 1850s, 160,000 to 200,000 blacks, constituting about 5 percent of the total slave population, worked in industry. A decade later there were more free blacks in the South than in the North, or 250,787 and 238,268 respectively. In the South, free blacks were concentrated in the cities where they worked as artisans. In 1902, Atlanta had 843 black mechanics and artisans, of this number 178 were carpenters and seventy-three masons. "The skilled Negro artisans, however were gradually being forced to relinquish their hold upon the trades in spite of a rise of their own contractors, but unskilled labor in building trades continued as a monopoly controlled by Negroes. This was due to several causes. In the first place, this work fell into the opprobrious category of Negro jobs."[6]

Du Bois and Dill found that before the downfall of slavery, white mechanics had been replaced almost entirely by the slave mechanics. "Many of the railroads in the South had their entire train crews, except the conductors, made up of the slaves – including engineers and firemen. The Georgia Central had inaugurated just such a movement, and had many engineers on its locomotives and Negro mechanists in its shops."[7]

In 1859, a petition submitted to the Atlanta City Council graphically illustrates the hostility and harassment that black entrepreneurs endured from white businesspersons. It also shows how whites subverted the free market to protect themselves from the competition of blacks. "We feel aggrieved as Southern citizens that your honorable body tolerates a Negro dentist (Rodrick Badger) in our midst; and in justice to ourselves and the community it ought to be abated. We the residents of Atlanta appeal to you for justice."[8]

Petitions such as these were designed to break the monopoly that black slaves and free laborers exercised in certain mechanical and skilled trades in Atlanta and Georgia, and to deny blacks an equal chance in the marketplace. In addition to pressuring state and local legislators into passing anti-black statutes that restricted and in some cases prohibited blacks from engaging in skilled trades, whites agitated for the passage of segregation laws, and incited riots to gain control of labor markets. Trade unions were segregated and commercial licensing laws were crafted to deny blacks access to specialized areas.

Black entrepreneurs were excluded de jure and de facto from white consumer markets, and in some cases even the black consumer markets. A few years ago, T.M. Alexander, one of Atlanta's successful senior black entrepreneurs, shared with this author the draft copy of his autobiography, *Beyond the Timber Line*.[9] In the course of our discussion, he recounted some of the darkest aspects of Jim Crow segregation, noting that blacks were racially excluded from some industries even when they intended to serve black clients. Not only did discrimination deny black entrepreneurs access to white consumers, he observed, it also denied them access to black consumers in certain lines of commerce. Alexander, Georgia's first licensed insurance agent, discusses these experiences in his autobiography.

Racism separated black entrepreneurs legally and psychologically from their natural customer base. For example, Alexander notes that in the 1930s, he had to fight on two fronts to be successful, against the "dubious practices" of would-be white competitors and for the acceptance of black consumers. "For many years," Alexander writes:

> blacks had been shrewdly taught to place their confidence in whites and to look with doubt and suspicion upon their own race. This was a sad but true fact of life that hampered many black companies. My white competitors would stress the unavoidable failures of black business in an effort to capture the black market. White salesmen of all kinds could enter large numbers of black homes with little sales resistance. I could not. Ironically, the white agents would enter black homes without the usual courtesy one would expect essential to good salesmanship.
>
> They kept their hats on, and they addressed members of the family by their first names.[10]

As a child growing up in the pre-civil rights Jacksonville, Florida, the author recalls the racial insults that occurred whenever white insurance agents sold home service life insurance policies door to door. On one occasion an agent indulged in the normal practice of addressing my mother by her first name. Fortunately, on this occasion my father was home. Dad ordered the agent out of our house and told him never to return. Eventually, the insurance company sent a more courteous white agent in his place. Unfortunately black agents employed by white-owned companies were rare during those days.

Becoming an agent, if one were black, was a difficult task. Once, Alexander decided to sell automobile policies to blacks because white-owned insurance companies would not provide blacks with liability insurance beyond the period that the car was being financed. As soon as the car was paid for, the policies of blacks were dropped. So Alexander decided to write policies on blacks if he could find a white insurance company willing to accept the risk. Upon approaching some of the major companies in the city, he explained that he had some very promising clients and was searching for a company where he could place insurance on a selected line of risk. On finding out Alexander's race, one agent replied, "Did you say you are a nigger?" and another remarked, "Sorry, I write a few niggers but they are good boys that I know or who are recommended by my friends. I can't have no nigger agents."[11]

White competitors also attempted to strip Alexander of his insurance license unlawfully, but eventually he became one of the most successful black businessmen in Atlanta. Blacks that dared to enter non-traditional industries experienced these racial encounters. From the ante-bellum period to modern civil rights era, whites used legal and extralegal means to restrict the competition of black entrepreneurs.

The Atlanta Public School System, the Georgia State Legislature and the Atlanta City Government (each funded by public tax dollars) played active and passive roles in perpetuating racial discrimination. It is widely recognized that education is one of the most important elements in the development of an entrepreneurial class, but Atlanta maintained a segregated and inferior school system for blacks until the 1960s. The legal support for this racism resided in the Georgia Legislature.

So in all walks of life, blacks faced racial segregation; in labor markets, housing, education, social services, and even in access to markets that served other blacks. This environment fostered mom and pop operations.

> It is not unreasonable to assume that during the nineteenth century and until the 1960's, prospective black businessmen were rather reluctant to start a business beyond the 'mom and pop' variety. For indeed, any large-scale enterprise would have been in all probability dependent in some way upon white suppliers and/or white consumers either or both of which would have probably proved hostile. Furthermore, black entrepreneurs faced the very real possibilities of receiving either physical harm or destruction of their property by antagonistic white competitors or bigots.[12]

Occasionally, racism in Atlanta was so perverse that more qualified black workers, employed at cheaper wages, were dismissed *en
masse* to make room for less qualified, higher paid white workers.
One example of this was when Atlanta's Sanitary Department
discharged all its black truck drivers and replaced them with white
drivers. Experienced black drivers were paid $60 per month, while
new white drivers were hired at a minimum wage of $100 per
month. This was not a unique occurrence:

> The Jacob Drug Company, a chain of 120 stores in Atlanta,
> had for thirty years employed black youth as messengers.
> On July 15, 1929, however, the 230 black messengers were
> discharged and the white youth to take their places were
> given an increase in pay of $3 per week, plus a regulation
> uniform. Similarly, between 1919 and 1929, black truck
> drivers for the Hormel Company, Swift Company, Cudahy
> Packing Company, Wilson Company, and White Provision
> Company were replaced with white drivers. The Georgia
> Baptist Hospital, one of the South's largest private hospi-
> tals, discharged its entire black work force and gave an
> increase in pay to the new white workers. The white
> patients, however, complained about the inexperience and
> inefficiency of the white workers and, after two months of
> trial and error, the black workers were called back. The
> black workers were given the same salary as before they
> were discharged even though the whites who replaced them
> were paid more during their short tenure.[13]

Education was separate and unequal

On 17 May 1954, the U.S. Supreme Court ruled that "separate
educational facilities are inherently unequal,"[14] but the Georgia
General Assembly resisted this decision. To preserve segregation, it
passed an Act that allowed the assembly to fund private schools with
taxpayers' money. Commenting on the amendment that was ratified
by 210,488 Georgia voters, Governor Herman Talmadge said:

> Despite efforts of the opposition to create a different issue,
> the people of Georgia have ratified an amendment to give
> the General Assembly of Georgia and the Governor power
> to preserve segregation in our schools.

I hope it will never become necessary to use the amendment, but this should put the Supreme Court of the United States and the people of this nation on notice that the people of Georgia are determined to preserve segregation.[15]

In 1955, Act 82 of Senate Bill Number 40 stipulated that "no State or local funds could be expended for public school purposes unless the white and Negro races were educated separately. . . . The law further provides that any official expending either state or local funds contrary to the provision of the 1955 Act would be guilty of a felony and personally liable for any amount so paid out as well as the possibility of two years imprisonment."[16]

In 1956 the General Assembly of Georgia declared the Supreme Court's decision "null and void," and a year later passed a resolution to impeach six members of the U.S. Supreme Court, charging them with "high crimes and misdemeanors" and with "sedition."[17]

Mark Huie notes that, in the fall of 1960, the Atlanta school system was finally ordered to desegregate. In 1961, there were only ten blacks in previously all-white schools; by 1966 this had increased to 9,328.

The University of Georgia was ordered to desegregate by the United States District Court for the Middle District of Georgia. When two blacks went to classes at the University on Wednesday, 11 January 1961, this was the first time in Georgia's history that "white and Negro students had knowingly sat together in a tax-supported institution of learning."[18]

Atlanta's old black bourgeoisie

By the beginning of the twentieth century, blacks in Atlanta had laid the foundation of a rich business tradition, despite the racism they encountered. Prominent family names associated with its growing black business sector included Rucker, Cunningham, Cater, Yates, Milton, Harper, Trent, Hopkins, Faulkner and Dobbs. John Wesley Dobbs coined the phrase "Sweet Auburn" to represent the vitality of the formerly white neighborhood that by the 1920s had become home to what some have claimed was the richest stretch of black-owned real estate in America. By 1911 "Atlanta had some two thousand black-owned establishments representing over a hundred types of business, including one bank, three insurance companies, 12 drugstores, 60 tailor shops, 83 barber shops, 85 groceries, 80 hack lines, and 125 drayage places."[19]

The business tradition in Atlanta was closely related to the six schools founded for blacks during the two decades after the Civil War. These schools now comprise the Atlanta University Center. They are Clark-Atlanta University [formerly Atlanta University (1867) and Clark College (1869)], Morehouse (1879), Spelman (1880), Morris Brown (1881), and the Interdenominational Theological Center (1883). By the 1920s, several of the most prominent black entrepreneurs on "Sweet Auburn" Avenue occupied faculty positions in the business and economics departments at the Atlanta University Center Schools.

Josephine Harreld Love, now a Detroit resident, was a child during the heyday of "Sweet Auburn" and recently shared her vivid recollection of the era in a letter to the author:

"I remember – reinforced by later references – the year that Lorimer Milton came to Atlanta! Probably I was around seven years old. . . .

Milton and Clayton Yates opened a combination pharmacy/soda fountain/post office sub-station that quickly reinforced the image of Auburn Avenue as headquarters for black business enterprise. It was already the setting for an assortment of service outlets – barber and beauty, cleaning, repair, and tailor shops, doctor, dentist, lawyer, and real estate offices, and secret order headquarters. Some were housed in pre-1920's office complexes built by the Odd Fellows. . . .

The Odd Fellows Building boasted a night club called the Roof Garden. Its front sidewalk served as platform for various soapbox personalities. Some of them, I am sure, among the nation's most colorful and compelling street orators. This could certainly be said about Benjamin Davis, Sr. and John Wesley Dobbs. . . .

Full-blown enterprise was abundantly in evidence on two sides of town – along the Auburn Avenue and Hunter-Mitchell Street corridors. Auburn Avenue had a bank, more than one insurance and savings and loan companies, a bookstore, optical shop in addition to varied outlets for personal care and professional service. There were three churches with larger congregations – Bethel A.M.E., Wheat Street and Ebenezer Baptist, a YMCA and a public library that Andrew Carnegie had built in response to the Atlanta Public Library system's failure to accommodate an African-American reading public. These institutions were in addition temples of culture sponsoring pageants, concert and lecture series and, to a degree, encouraged socio-political activism. . . .

These persons' stories and those of numbers of others are the metaphors for today's African American business success stories.

Strides taken in Atlanta's subsequent undertakings in upward mobility move across a foundation laid by earlier business and political pioneers . . . . None was, as too often pictured, unlettered, ungainly, incompetent in public office. They were instead from all accounts uncommonly astute, dynamic players in a post-Civil War drama."[20]

The vigor of Atlanta's black business class during the early part of the twentieth century contrasts with how the city treated these businesspersons. That the city did not award a contract to a black-owned business until 1973 says more about the rigidity of its racism than it says about the capability of black-owned businesses.

Rigid segregation barriers in the private sector matched the exclusion of black businesses from public-sector procurement. This situation forced black-owned businesses to rely almost exclusively on black customers and clients and to channel their commercial operations in a very narrow range of industries, usually associated with personal service and retail activities. The success stories notwithstanding, the lack of equal access to the general market virtually guaranteed that most black businesses would be little more than mom and pop operations.

Until affirmative action programs were implemented, it was impossible for black contractors, architects and construction managers to serve as prime contractors or subcontractors on major public works projects. Affirmative action programs created opportunities that allowed these entrepreneurs to accumulate the financial wherewithal and track record to break out of this straitjacket. As blacks entered more dynamically growing industries, the character of their businesses changed accordingly.

Between 1972 and 1992, Atlanta's black-owned retail establishments decreased by 14 percentage points from 27 percent of all black-owned businesses to 13 percent. In contrast, selected service industries increased from 31 to 51 percent. These changes reflect the decline of mom and pop operations and the emergence of a new entrepreneur.

The creation of public-sector opportunities required the dismantling of the discriminatory apparatus at City Hall. This apparatus had excluded blacks for an entire century. Dismantling racism was only the first step. Strong measures were needed to compensate blacks for past injustices and these measures required a bold affirmative action initiative.

5

WHAT CAUSES THE LAG IN BLACK ENTREPRENEURSHIP?

Understanding the entrepreneur

The traits and activities of entrepreneurs have been studied for more than two hundred years. Individuals such as Richard Cantillion (c.1730), Jean-Baptiste Say (c.1810), Karl Marx (c.1867), Alfred Marshall (c.1890), Joseph Schumpeter (c.1910) and in recent times Harvey Leibenstein (c.1970) have all contributed significantly to this body of knowledge. Today, research on entrepreneurship is growing in popularity in several academic areas of study including psychology, economics, management, sociology and anthropology. The traits identified as most common to entrepreneurs are risk-bearing behavior, the coordination of productive resources, introduction of innovation and creativity, and the provision of capital. Oliver Clayton argues that entrepreneurs must:

> Be aggressive, be competitive, be goal-oriented, be egocentric, make decisions, be an achiever very earlier in life, be a loner in your final decision, put family and friends second to business, be an opportunist, do not be security-oriented, be persistent, have determination, be an optimist (to an extreme), have desire to achieve, be hyperactive mentally, be a dreamer, be a calculated risk-taker, want power, learn from previous mistakes, be a perfectionist and be intuitive.[1]

In a study of 217 minority entrepreneurs, Hirsch and Brush identified the factors that provide the greatest motivation for minorities to enter entrepreneurship. In order of importance they are: achievement, opportunity, job satisfaction, independence, money, economic necessity, career security, power, and status. Similarly, the factors that create the biggest barriers in business

73

start-ups are: obtaining lines of credit, lack of business training, lack of management experience, weak collateral position, lack of experience in financial planning, lack of guidance and counseling, lack of experience in hiring outside services, and lack of respect.[2]

To understand an ethnic business, one must examine the three interactive components it is built on.[3]

1   Opportunity structures, which includes favorable market conditions, the ability to provide products and services beyond ethnic markets, the ease of access to business opportunities, competition and government policies.
2   Group characteristics, including selective migration, culture, aspirations, ethnic and social networks, organizing capabilities, ability to mobilize resources, and the extent to which government facilitates or constrains resource acquisition.
3   The strategies emerging from the interaction between opportunity structures and group characteristics.

It is interesting to juxtapose all of the above-cited criteria with the historical environment experienced by blacks. Until the last few decades, many were excluded from jobs, labor unions, and business and country clubs because of their race. They were educated in second-class schools and lived in residentially segregated, poorer neighborhoods. In the labor market, they occupied a disproportionate share of the low-skilled secondary-sector jobs and were more than twice as likely to be unemployed. Access to capital and credit institutions was low and often non-existent. Similarly, black-owned businesses experienced discrimination in the private sector and were virtually excluded from public-sector contracting and procurement until affirmative action plans were instituted. Clearly, such an environment is antithetical to nurturing the personality traits, capital resources, and human capital attributes that are essential for successful entrepreneurship.

As a result, in 1960, most black-owned businesses could be described as mom and pop operations. That year, the 46,400 businesses represented 2.4 percent of the nation's total. More striking, 57 percent were engaged in small retail activities that served a black clientele. By contrast, black businesses serving the general market were rare. The perverse incentives and lack of opportunities available to blacks constrained their market and industry diversification. Reasonable opportunities and normal returns for risk taking were simply not available to the black business sector, and its evolution reflected these constraints.

Things did not begin to change on a noticeable scale until the late 1970s and early 1980s. Government contracting was pivotal in this change because of the difficulties blacks encountered in gaining access to non-minority markets in the private sector. So the seeds of the current diversification and growing capacity of black businesses can be traced in part to local, state and federal procurement opportunities. In 1987 total federal procurement with minorities was $7.5 billion. This was equivalent to 10 percent of the $77.8 billion in gross revenue received by all minority firms and it still does not include state and local government procurement with minorities.

Between 1960 and the early 1980s a significant shift occurred in the character of black-owned businesses. Table 5.1 indicates that in 1960, most self-employed black business-persons were in personal services (28.9 percent), retail (25.4 percent), and construction (16.7 percent). By 1980, this distribution had changed dramatically. In particular, black self-employment in personal service industries declined by 49 percent during the twenty-year period while retailers posted a zero growth. In contrast, the fastest growth areas for the self-employed were wholesaling, business services, finance, insurance and real estate and, to a more limited extent, manufacturing.

Table 5.1 Time trends in the relative incidence of self-employment, by industry group. Percentage of all minorities self-employed in various industries, 1960–80

Industry	1960	1980	% change
Construction	16.7%	16.5%	−1.2%
Manufacturing	4.1%	6.0%	46.3%
Transportation, communication, utilities	3.9%	6.0%	53.8%
Wholesale	1.7%	3.6%	111.8%
Retail	25.4%	25.4%	0.0%
Finance, insurance, real estate	1.4%	4.0%	185.7%
Business services	2.4%	6.6%	175.0%
Repair services	5.2%	6.9%	32.7%
Personal services	28.9%	14.7%	−49.1%
Other services	10.3%	10.3%	0.0%
Total	100.0%	100.0%	–

Source: Timothy Bates, "Self-Employed Minorities: Traits and Trends," *Social Science Quarterly* Vol. 68, 1987, p.541.

Between 1977 and 1982, as black-owned businesses grew by 46.7 percent. This was four times the growth rate of all US businesses. However, this growth rate was not even for example, personal service firms declined while business service firms thrived. Additionally, the receipts of the latter doubled and the share of employment they accounted for increased from 8 percent to 14 percent of total employment in all black firms.[4]

Despite the changing dynamics of black-owned businesses, these firms still account for a rather insignificant share of overall commercial activity. As of 1987, the SMOBE indicated that the 424,165 black-owned firms accounted for 3.1 percent of all U.S. firms and 1 percent of all U.S. business receipts. The average gross revenue per firm of $46,593 is exactly 25 percent of the gross annual revenue of businesses owned by white men and 32 percent of all U.S. firms. Blacks have smaller annual revenues than Hispanics ($58,555) and Asians ($93,222). Table 5.2 reflects the representation of black and minority businesses in all industries in 1987. The table gives the number, gross revenue, and average revenue of all U.S. firms, all minority firms and black-owned firms. It also gives the percent of total revenue in each industry accounted for by minority and black businesses in the industry. In all industries, black-owned businesses receive a much smaller percent of the total revenue than their representation in that industry. The largest representation of black-owned businesses occurs in the transportation and utilities industry (6.2 percent).

Starting a successful business

Feldman, Koberg and Dean have examined the process by which minority entrepreneurs start businesses. Their survey of 172 minority respondents was compared to the responses of 1,756 non-minority respondents surveyed in the National Federation of Independent Business study. There were two major objectives of the comparison. First, to determine if there are systematic differences in the path to business ownership between the groups. Second, to determine if there are significant differences in the backgrounds, characteristics, motivation and traits between the groups. The results are very revealing (see Table 5.3).

For non-minority respondents, the primary paths to business ownership are: starting a business (49 percent), purchasing an existing non-family business (28 percent), and inheriting a family business (15 percent). By contrast, for blacks these percentages are: starting a business (94.3 percent), purchasing an existing

Table 5.2 Comparison of average annual receipts by business category (1987)

Industry	Number of firms	Total receipts (000)	Average receipts ($)	% of total U.S.	% minority & black (U.S.)
Total U.S.	13,695,480	1,994,808,000	145,654	94.9%[a]	–
Total minority	1,213,750	77,840,000	64,132		–
Total black	424,165	19,762,876	46,593		–
Agriculture & mining (U.S.)	478,042	35,669,000	74,615	3.5%	100.0%
Minority	38,477	1,475,372	38,344		8.0%
Black	7,658	270,813	35,456		1.6%
Construction (U.S.)	1,651,102	232,772,000	140,980	12.1%	100.0%
Minority	107,650	6,903,022	64,125		6.5%
Black	36,763	2,174,394	59,146		2.2%
Manufacturing (U.S.)	432,971	226,824,000	523,878	3.2%	100.0%
Minority	29,200	3,961,128	132,572		6.7%
Black	8,004	1,023,104	127,824		1.8%
Transportation/utilities (U.S.)	592,751	76,335,000	128,781	4.3%	100.0%
Minority	76,229	3,665,682	48,088		12.9%
Black	36,958	1,573,342	42,571		6.2%
Wholesale (U.S.)	439,200	29,826,400	679,108	3.2%	100.0%
Minority	26,432	7,950,013	300,772		6.0%
Black	5,519	1,327,479	240,529		1.3%
Retail (U.S.)	2,241,494	544,768,000	243,038	16.4%	100.0%
Minority	226,140	26,903,914	118,970		10.1%
Black	66,229	5,889,654	88,929		3.0%
Finance/insurance/real estate (U.S.)	1,227,215	123,710,000	100,806	9.0%	100.0%
Minority	76,442	2,759,980	36,106		6.2%
Black	26,989	804,252	29,799		2.2%
Service (U.S.)	5,937,671	417,105,000	70,247	43.4%	100.0%
Minority	562,559	21,990,719	30,091		9.5%
Black	209,547	6,120,084	29,206		3.3%

Source: United States Commission on Minority Business Development, Final Report (Washington, DC: U.S. Government Printing Office, 1992).
Notes [a] Total percent of industries in the U.S. does not include non-classified industries.

Table 5.3 The path to business ownership

| Group | 1979 NFIB Study (n = 1,756) | Minority owners (n = 172) | Subsamples of minority owners[a] | | | | |
			Asians (n = 18)	Native Americans (n = 18)	Hispanics (n = 88)	Blacks (n = 35)
Started the business	49.0%	87.7%	88.9%	88.9%	85.2%	94.3%
Purchased the business (not from family)	28.0%	6.5%	11.1%	0	8.0%	2.9%
Inherited business/purchased from member of family	15.0%	4.1%	0	5.6%	4.5%	2.9%
Promoted or brought in by other owners	5.0%	1.2%	0	5.6%	0	0
Other path	3.0%	1.2%	0	0	2.3%	0

Source: Howard Feldman et al., "Minority Small Business Owners and Their Paths to Ownership," Journal of Small Business Management, Vol. 29, Oct. 1991, p.20.

Notes
[a] Thirteen respondents indicated "other" as their race, indicating a mixture of two or more minority groups in their background.

non-family business (2.9 percent), and inheriting a family business (2.9 percent). For all minority owners these percentages are: starting a business (87.7 percent), purchasing an existing non-family business (6.5 percent) and inheriting a family business (4.1 percent). (See Table 5.3.)[5]

Virtually every study of minority entrepreneurs finds that a major problem in starting and operating a business is obtaining lines of credit. The Feldman, Koberg and Dean study provides evidence that supports this view. In particular, the significant differences in the path to business formation suggest that capital may indeed be a major problem for blacks.

During the initial stages of a firm's development, entrepreneurs rely heavily upon their personal wealth and that of their family and friends. Bates and Dunham find that entry into self-employment is strongly correlated with household net worth exceeding $100,000. Therefore, factors that influence household wealth will also influence business start-ups.[6] The latest study of the characteristics of business owners by the Census Bureau indicates that non-minority men receive 13 percent of their original capital from family and friends while black business owners receive 10.7 percent from such sources. Likewise, non-minority men borrow 16 percent of their initial capital from commercial banks while black business owners get 9.5 percent of their initial capital through such channels.

The differences in the rate of entrepreneurship between blacks and other ethnic groups have been found to be attributable mainly to the lower business start-up rate for blacks, and not to a higher failure rate. Richard Stevens has shown that failure rates across ethnic groups do not vary significantly. For example, they are 12.3 percent for blacks, 13.9 percent for Hispanics and 12.3 percent for Asians. What varies are formation rates: 14.9 percent, 17.2 percent and 20.7 percent respectively for blacks, Hispanics and Asians.[7]

A 1986 study by the U.S. Department of Commerce examines the minority business financing issue. Thirteen hundred businesses were surveyed, and about 400 of these were minority-owned. These were all successful businesses as measured by their length of time in operation, gross sales of greater than $500,000 and profits of greater than $34,000 before taxes. The characteristics of minority and non-minority business owners were similar. In fact, black business owners in the survey had education, experience and credit ratings which were almost identical to non-minorities (see Table 5.4).

Four characteristics were found to be correlated with success in obtaining capital: the amount of equity seed capital, the legal form

Table 5.4 Characteristics of minority and non-minority firms and owners in the JACA sample, 1983 (% except as noted)

	Business owned by			
	Non-minorities	Asians	Blacks	Hispanics
Characteristics of business				
Mean year business was started	1963	1968	1967	1967
Form of ownership				
Sole proprietor	51.9	48.4	51.3	42.1
Joint co-proprietor	1.2	4.9	1.7	0.9
Partner	4.3	4.1	1.7	5.3
Corporation	42.6	42.6	45.3	51.8
Mean size of firm with employees (employees per firm)				
1980	8.4	6.5	6.0	5.4
1983	9.7	8.3	7.7	8.3
Credit rating of firm				
Excellent	66.0	70.7	66.1	41.3
Good	19.9	19.8	20.0	37.6
Average	7.8	8.6	9.6	14.7
Poor	2.0	0.0	2.6	6.4
Characteristics of owners				
Work experience (mean years in related areas before business)				
Ownership	5.6	3.3	5.3	4.3
Blue collar	5.2			
Managerial	22.0			
Mean years of school completed	15.2	15.1	13.9	15.6
Type of education				
Some college	79.0	76.5	70.4	84.0
Business courses	51.5	38.5	51.3	51.3
Vocational courses	44.9	41.7	51.3	57.1
Willingness and ability to work long hours (mean hours worked)				
Primary job	50.3	53.2	51.2	51.8
Second job	22.1	30	27.4	28.3
Personal credit rating				
Excellent	74.5	75.2	69.3	52.7
Good	14.5	17.9	18.4	25.0
Average	6.1	1.7	7.9	12.5
Poor	2.1	1.1	3.5	8.9
Mean personal net worth of owner	$53,930	$91,376	$51,466	$62,433

Source: U.S. Department of Commerce, *State of Small Business*, (Washington DC: U.S. Government Publications Office, 1986), pp.242–3.

of organization, credit rating or debt ratio, and length of time in operation. The success rate in obtaining loans was similar for all groups except blacks. To test whether racial discrimination affected success in obtaining loans, a regression analysis was conducted. The study found that "black business owners experience a lower success rate because of race, while Asian and Hispanic businesses encountered no measurable racial discrimination."[8]

The factors contributing to success can be classified into individual and group-specific elements, and environmental elements. Listed among the former are: (1) the diversity of the group's social class structures and, in particular, the size and character of its middle class; (2) the human capital endowment of entrepreneurs, including such factors as education, business and management related experience, attitude towards risk-taking, and interaction with role models; (3) the availability of group social capital and business support networks, specifically resources within the group from family, friends or other ethnic organizations; (4) internal business practices, for example management skills, business location, strategic planning, and operational technology; and (5), an individual's ability to assume risk and/or finance his or her operations.

Environmental factors consist of: (1) the accessibility of debt and equity capital; (2) the extent to which racial discrimination lowers the opportunities available to black entrepreneurs; (3) the accessibility of the public and private sectors; (4) support of the social and political environment including such programs as affirmative action and small business assistance; (5) labor force quality, and the size, income status and accessibility of the ethnic and non-ethnic markets; and (6) the compatibility of the local infrastructure to support business development.[9] To improve the rate of black entrepreneurship, advances must be made in each of these areas.

Conclusion

William Baumol states that if we want to explain why some economies have grown significantly and others have remained relatively stagnant, we must look at "differences in the availability of entrepreneurial talent and in the motivational mechanism which drives them on."[10] The really big differences in economic life are highly correlated with the presence or absence of an effective class of entrepreneurs, Baumol notes. So, to understand why the economic status of blacks has lagged behind that of whites, we should examine the differences in their respective environments and how the entrepreneurs in each racial group have adapted to and been affected by their environment. This chapter has examined the set of incentives and opportunities that have confronted blacks historically and how they have responded to them.

Incentives, opportunities and rewards for risk-taking are fundamental driving forces of entrepreneurship. In environments where these ingredients are absent or distorted, abnormalities usually appear in the associated class of entrepreneurs. For example, consider the differences that have occurred over the last fifty years between the entrepreneurs of East Germany and West Germany. The presence of so many successful entrepreneurs in the West and so few in the East is traceable to the different opportunities and incentives in their respective environments. Both share the same cultural history, but the communist environment in the East caused a different outcome than the free market environment in the West. When communism collapsed, entrepreneurship activity re-emerged in the East. Now businesses in the East are beginning to teach lessons to the West about efficient business practices.

Some researchers argue that the wide disparities in business formation are due to differences in entrepreneurial propensities among ethnic groups.[11] In doing so, they usually fail to account for the factor that is fundamental to entrepreneurial behavior, the return for risk-taking. The set of incentives within a given environment plays a key role in shaping the character of the entrepreneurs within that environment. Where there are appropriate opportunities and rewards, entrepreneurship usually breaks through cultural constraints. We have shown how this is taking place in Atlanta. In fact, Atlanta's experience is the best example of what can happen when opportunities are available. The growing success of black-owned businesses in Atlanta and other cities across the country in response to new opportunities is shattering the myth that entrepreneurship is a cultural phenomenon. The decline of racial barriers creates social and economic opportunities and it opens social and business networks that are crucial to developing successful businesses.

6

A JUDICIAL COMMISSION ON STRICT SCRUTINY IS NEEDED

The twists and turns of affirmative action legislation

The U.S. Commission on Civil Rights defines affirmative action as "any measure, beyond simple termination of a discriminatory practice, adopted to correct or compensate for past or present discrimination or to prevent discrimination from recurring in the future." President Lyndon Johnson first used the term in a 1965 executive order committing the federal government to providing equal opportunity in employment.

In 1981, the federal government awarded only 3.4 percent of its total procurement to minorities. In Richmond, Virginia, the focal point of the Croson Decision, minorities received only 0.67 percent of $24.6 million in procurement contracts between 1978 and 1983. In 1989 in St. Louis, Missouri, minorities received only 2.2 percent of all city contracting and procurement. Finally, in the City of Atlanta in 1973, minorities received only 0.13 percent of all contracting and procurement.

The experiences of black business owners in Richmond, St. Louis and Atlanta matched those of owners in dozens of other cities across the nation. Discrimination in public-sector procurement denied minorities equal access to commercial opportunities. These practices persisted even when qualified black entrepreneurs were available. Since the Bakke Decision in 1978,[1] the Supreme Court has grappled with determining the circumstances wherein race-based remedies are permissible. In this regard, the Court's rulings have not always been independent of social influences.[2]

In 1977, in the case of *Fullilove* v. *Klutznick*, the Court recognized that Congress has unique powers and the ability to impose race-based remedies. The issue at hand was the constitutionality of federally mandated set-asides. More than ten years later, the Croson Decision drew upon the premise established in the case of *Wygant* v. *Jackson Board of Education* and required state and local entities to meet the strict scrutiny standard. The Court varied from this course in the *Metro Broadcasting* v. *FCC* decision by ruling that remedies based on race are permissible if they serve a greater social good. But the Adarand Decision reversed this course and dissolved the unique powers of Congress to impose race-based remedies without specific findings of discrimination. The current consensus on the Court is that local, state and federal agencies can implement race-based remedies, but only if they satisfy the strict scrutiny standard.

Society adopts affirmative action

The modern civil rights movement began in 1955 with the Montgomery bus boycott. This struggle drew strength from the 1954 Supreme Court decision that declared racially separate educational systems inherently unequal. The fight for equal justice in society occasioned several important judicial and legislative decisions. For example, in its 1961 decision in the case of *Boynton* v. *Commonwealth of Virginia*, the Supreme Court ruled that discrimination against interstate travelers in bus terminals was illegal. In 1964 and 1965 the Civil Rights Act and the Voting Rights Act were passed. These are two of the most important civil rights legislative acts this century. Over the next twenty years these acts were followed by a series of federal acts and provisions aimed at breaking down discriminatory barriers and accelerating the participation of blacks in the American mainstream.

In 1965 President Johnson signed Executive Order 10925. This Order marked the first time that the federal government made reference to affirmative action. President Johnson signed Executive Order 11246 in September 1965. This Order, along with detailed regulations passed in 1968 and amendments added in 1970 and 1971, outlines with specificity the government's affirmative action policy. It provided the basis of the federal government's contract compliance program by introducing important concepts such as under-utilization, availability, good faith efforts, and goals and timetables. One of the most important clauses of this Order points out that procedures without effort to make them work are meaningless; and effort, undirected by specific and meaningful procedures, is inadequate.[3]

Executive Order 11246 was implemented in the employment

arena. It required companies with over fifty employees and more than $50,000 in business with the federal government to develop goals and timetables for achieving a more diverse workforce. The Philadelphia Plan, implemented by Nixon, is considered to be the first enforceable affirmative action plan. This plan required companies competing for $4 billion in federal projects in Philadelphia to make a good faith effort to hire minorities by setting flexible goals for hiring minority workers. Sanctions were imposed on companies that could not show good faith hiring efforts.[4]

If utilization is below that which is reasonably expected by the available labor pool, specific hiring goals and timetables were mandated to correct the under-utilization. The use of goals and timetables was held to be constitutional under Title II.[5] Presently, 90,000 firms are affected by this order; these firms employ 25 million workers.[6]

In 1969, Nixon issued Executive Order 11458 establishing the Minority Business Development Agency (MBDA) of the U.S. Department of Commerce. A subsequent Order, 11625 strengthened the MBDA further. The country's statutory attempt to use racial preferences in the administration of public works contracting was implemented in 1977 when Congress passed the Public Works Employment Act. This Act was amended by a minority business enterprise provision introduced by Representative Parren Mitchell and Senator Edward Brooke. This Act provided $4 billion in public works funds to states and localities but it also mandated that 10 percent of such funds be set-aside for minorities, i.e. blacks, Hispanics, Asians and Native Americans.[7]

Racial mandates operate in a number of ways. The pure set-aside (Type 1) mandates that a certain percentage of the total number or dollar value of contracts be reserved exclusively for minorities or women. States and localities seldom use this type of affirmative action policy. Perhaps the most commonly used affirmative action plan is the sub-contractor goal program (Type 2). This requires that a certain percentage of a prime contractor's award be expended (subcontracted) with minority or women vendors. However, this method is not suitable for categories of procurement that cannot be efficiently subcontracted, such as office supplies and equipment and other commodities. A variation on the subcontractor method is the joint venture (Type 3). In this regard, a majority and a minority prime contractor form a joint agreement with the minority firm participating to the extent of the mandated goal. This type of arrangement is typically used on the largest of contracts and is feasible only when minority or women firms have the appropriate capacity. Another variation is the bid preference (Type 4). Bid preferences usually operate by taking the lowest non-minority bid and inflating it upward by the stipulated percent of the preference. If the minority or women firm is the lowest bidder after the adjustment, then it is the recipient of the award. The award is made at the pre-adjustment bid. This method is used most often in situations where commodities and supplies are procured because of the economies of large-scale operations in these areas. These economies allow large establishments to be more competitive bidders. A final variation is when a majority firm is given a stipulated bonus for using a minority subcontractor (Type 5). That bonus may be a percentage amount or a dollar amount and the minority firm need not be the lowest bidding subcontractor.

In the 1971 decision involving *Griggs* v. *Duke Power Co.*, a unanimous Supreme Court ruled that a finding of discrimination is not dependent upon a showing of the intent to discriminate. Instead, it was only sufficient to show that practices, which were non-discriminatory on the surface, had a disparate or dispropor-tionate impact on one racial group. This opened the door for a number of affirmative action remedies and aided the evolution of minority preference programs.

The Wygant decision paves the way for Croson

The previously discussed Fullilove case concluded that minority preference programs enacted by the federal government are not subject to the strict scrutiny standard. Instead, such programs only need to be rationally related to an important governmental interest. Six years later the Court once again visited the constitutionality of an affirmative action program. Only this time, its decision paved the way for the Croson standard.

The road to the Croson Decision was paved by the 1986 Supreme Court case involving a challenge to an educational seniority system, *Wygant* v. *Jackson Board of Education*.[8] In Wygant, a collective bargaining agreement to correct the under representa-tion of minority teachers was struck between the teachers union and the Jackson School Board. The agreement provided that in the case of layoffs, those teachers with the most seniority will be retained except when the percentage of the minority teachers laid off exceeds the percentage of minority teachers employed. When some non-minority tenured teachers, having more seniority than probationary minority teachers, were laid off, the School Board decided not to adhere to the collective bargaining agreement and laid off probationary minority teachers instead.

The teachers union and two minority teachers filed suit in state court claiming the breach of agreement violated the Equal Protection Clause of the Civil Rights Act. The state court determined that there had not been a history of overt discrimination by the school system but nevertheless upheld the collective bargaining agreement on the grounds that it sought to remedy past societal discrimination.

On appeal, the federal court ruled that a finding of past discrimination was not necessary for the implementation of racial preferences. Instead, a finding of societal discrimination and the desire to provide role models for minority students justified the layoff provision constitutionally. However, the Supreme Court, in a five to four plurality, reversed these lower court rulings and stipulated that racial classifications must be justified by demonstrating that a "compelling governmental interest" exists. Further, the remedy chosen must be narrowly tailored. Justice Stevens dissented. He argued that the affirmative action plan was voluntarily adopted by the union membership and that it served a valid public purpose.[9] In contrast, Justice Powell argued that the justification for minority role models was not compelling and if allowed could support an open-ended remedy that is not related to any particularized findings. As such, the plan was not narrowly tailored.

The Wygant decision established unequivocally that evidence of prior discrimination is a "prerequisite for any racially-based state remedial action. The Supreme Court viewed societal discrimination alone as insufficient to justify classifications based on race."[10] Wygant marked the first time that the Fourteenth Amendment was used to benefit plaintiffs who were white. The opinion expressed by a plurality of justices would subsequently find its way into the Croson case. The concept of intermediate scrutiny, which requires a rational relationship, gave way to a strict scrutiny standard for race-based remedies by states and localities.

Conclusion

The Croson decision can be reduced to the following essential questions. Do qualified, willing and able minority firms experience a significant disparity in the value of contracts they receive relative to their proportion of all contractors? If a significant disparity exists, is a portion of it attributable to discrimination? In the absence of discrimination, would minorities have received a significantly larger percentage of the total value of contracting and procurement? Are race conscious goals restricted to vendors that have experienced discrimination? Can the goal be achieved through means other than race conscious measures? Will goals be waived in the absence of qualified, willing and able minority vendors? Is the remedy temporary?

Racial preferences may be implemented if the disparity study underlying the program has addressed the specific questions listed above. But providing a straight forward answer to these simple questions has proven to be next to impossible because no uniform guidelines exist. Generalized findings, such as those presented by the City of Richmond in defense of its program, are not sufficient. Minority business programs have spent millions of dollars attempting to comply with this standard. Nevertheless, they are being subjected to legal challenges despite the costly and elaborate studies upon which they are based. For blacks to enjoy the constitutional rights of equal protection and due process, and receive appropriate remedies for past inequities, strict scrutiny must become more than just a theory whose parameters can be molded to fit any partisan political persuasion. It is imperative that there be established a Judicial Commission on Strict Scrutiny so that objective, uniform and fair criteria for the conduct of disparity studies and operation of affirmative action programs will exist.

Every agency now faces a triple jeopardy: they must pay for a disparity study, incur legal expenses "when", not if, the program is sued, and they often have to pay compensatory damages. To avoid this, the evidentiary standard needs to be clarified by an independent body. The Supreme Court failed to address this issue in the Croson and Adarand Decisions. Therefore, a Judicial Commission is needed. The best way to "mend affirmative action and not end it" is to make sure that strict scrutiny ceases to be "strict in theory and fatal in fact."

7

"TWENTY BY TEN"

A strategy for black business and employment growth in the next century

The economic status of blacks has improved during this current period of growth. Poverty among blacks is at the lowest level since the government began tracking the figures in 1959, and over the latest year the average household income of blacks increased by 3.6 percent while the income of whites increased by 2.2 percent. But these improvements bring to mind the metaphor of the half-filled glass – that is, the glass may be interpreted as being half-full or half-empty. Consider this: even though average household income among blacks has improved, it is still only 63 percent of that of whites, while 30 percent of black families still live below the poverty line. Finally, while the rate of unemployment among whites is 3.7 percent, it is 9.2 percent for blacks.

In the 1970s, blacks comprised 20 percent of all unemployed workers. Twenty years later they comprise the same percentage even though they constitute only 11.2 percent of the labor force and the economy is experiencing the longest peacetime expansion in history. Indeed, racial disparities have not changed significantly over the last twenty years. As long as the employment of blacks is assumed to "trickle down" from general full-employment policies, racial disparities will remain.

Suppose, however, that there are two types of company in the economy, Type A and Type B. Suppose in Type A companies, 10.5 out of every 100 workers are black. By contrast, in Type B companies eighty out of every 100 workers are black. Now if we want to create jobs for blacks, what is the solution? Simple – create more Type B companies. In general, about 80 percent of all employees in black-owned firms are black while in the economy as a whole, only about 10.5 percent of all employed workers are black.

We have previously shown that in Atlanta the most successful

African-American-owned firms employ a workforce that is about 80 percent black. In addition, these firms locate overwhelmingly in African-American communities, and 21 percent of their employees are from low-income inner city neighborhoods. The inescapable conclusion of this chapter is that if the government or society wishes to increase African-American employment and reduce the economic distress of inner-city neighborhoods, the most effective way to accomplish this is by promoting the growth of African-American-owned businesses. This chapter summarizes the stages of evolution of black-owned businesses over the last quarter century and argues for a strategy of black business and employment growth called "Twenty by Ten."

In plain language, Twenty by Ten calls for the government and private sector to pursue policies that are designed to create a sufficient number of black-owned firms such that their combined employment capacity will be equal to 20 percent of the black labor force by the year 2010: hence Twenty by Ten.

The stages of black business growth over the last quarter century

The major stages of black-owned business development over the last quarter century are as follows: (1) the decline of the first generation of black-owned businesses; (2) the emergence of the second generation of black-owned businesses; and (3), the emergence of the leading edge of the third generation of black-owned businesses. In characterizing black business transitions in this manner one should not get the impression that the traits of each new transition are broadly diffused among all black-owned businesses. The transitions are instead meant to identify the leading edge of change that is taking place and that appears to represent a qualitatively new but sustainable development.

1 Decline of the first generation of black-owned businesses

The best way to describe this transition is to call it the decline of "mom and pop." As noted previously, during the 1970s there occurred a rather significant transition in the industry composition of black-owned businesses. In particular, the relative share of establishments and gross revenue represented by traditional personal service and retail enterprises declined rather significantly. These changes coincided with the desegregation of society and the growing movement of middle- and upper-income blacks to the suburbs. The continued decline in the infrastructure of inner cities that started with the urban rebellions of the 1960s accelerated this movement to the suburbs. At the same time major chain stores and fast-food franchises, convenience stores, drug stores, commercial dry cleaners and one-stop gas stations moved into black communities and replaced many black-owned personal service and retail establishments. Now, establishments that had heretofore constituted the core of black businesses were losing their customer base to population dispersion, and they were facing stiffer competition for black consumers' dollars in markets that were formerly black or "protected", to borrow a phrase from Andrew Brimmer.

Tim Bates noted that, in 1972, 64 percent of black-owned businesses were concentrated in eight traditional industries: these were personal services (34,693 firms), miscellaneous retail (16,005), special trades contracting (15,616), eating and drinking places (14,346), food stores (11,887), business services (10,472), trucking and warehousing (9,938), and gas stations (6,579). In contrast, among firms that began operation between 1976 and 1982, only 10 percent were in personal services but 25 percent were in skill-intensive industries such as business services.

The changing character of black-owned businesses mirrored changes in the black population. Not only did the spatial location of the black population change, but their endowment of business related human capital also changed. Specifically, large numbers of blacks pursued business education at mainstream universities and major corporations undertook affirmative measures to recruit more blacks into management and professional positions. More than ever before, blacks accumulated the educational and managerial experience needed to establish dynamic businesses.

In short, while mom and pop enterprises were dying, a new generation of black-owned businesses was emerging. The owners of this new generation of businesses are young, well educated and experienced in business affairs. As a result, they established businesses in industries such as computer sales and services, architectural and engineering services, management and public relations, consulting and a host of business-related services.

When the new generation of black entrepreneurs operated in traditional industries, such as construction contracting, they moved their enterprises to a scale of operation that was previously impossible. To do this they relied on public sector contracting opportunities created by affirmative action programs in minority procurement.

Despite the fact that members of the new generation of black entrepreneurs were well educated, skilled and experienced, they still lacked access to markets in the private sector and in the public sector where minority business programs were not established. More importantly, they lacked access to debt and equity capital. But in the late 1970s the various federal departments and agencies enacted minority contracting programs. A turning point occurred in 1977 when the Public Works Employment Act mandated that 10 percent of its funds that were channeled to local public works projects be earmarked for minority businesses. During this period, the federal government made the biggest push for minority business inclusion. By contrast, little or nothing was happening in the private sector or at state and local governmental levels.

One noticeable characteristic of black-owned businesses of this era is that they relied on raising debt rather than equity capital as a source of growth. Pride in ethnic ownership took precedence over growth strategies that diffused ownership and control.

2 The second generation of black-owned businesses

By the 1980s many local governments followed the federal government's lead and initiated set-asides and other minority business procurement programs. Then, following the Fullilove Decision of 1980, local and state governments implemented these programs on a wide scale. These programs eventually became the lifeblood of many successful black entrepreneurs by providing them access to new markets and allowing them to expand their market shares. Government revenue constituted a comparatively more stable source income to businesses that had limited access to private capital markets, and allowed black entrepreneurs to operate on a scale that would have been impossible otherwise. Finally, these programs forced black and non-black firms into working relationships and partnerships. In short, affirmative action programs opened new horizons for black businesses. As a result, blacks were increasingly attracted out of the corporate sector and into business ventures.

Today, some of the most successful second-generation black-owned businesses have been able to establish strategic alliances with majority-owned firms. This has improved their success in the public sector and in some cases created opportunities in the private sector. Following the lead of local governments, some major corporations initiated affirmative action programs of their own. Many of these took the form of either franchise operations or procurement contracting. So by the late 1980s and early 1990s, a new generation of black-owned businesses had emerged in metropolitan areas across the country.

The successful businesses of this new generation achieved a scale of operation that was extremely large in comparison to businesses of the first generation, but their growth appeared to be constrained by their dependency on government contracting. In Atlanta we found that the average revenue of most successful second-generation businesses is $606,208. About 25 percent of these businesses earned more than this average. At the same time about one-third or better of their revenue is from government contracting.

The spatial location of these second-generation businesses mirrors the dispersion of the black population. Specifically, most are still located in predominately black neighborhoods even when they are in the suburbs. But regardless of where they locate, their work-force is overwhelmingly black.

Following the Croson Decision in 1989, the minority business programs that fueled the growth of the new generation came under attack, and this assault continues unfettered today. It is fair to say that the character and existence of affirmative action programs are changing rapidly. Under the guise of strict scrutiny, the lower courts and circuit courts are striking one blow after another at these programs.

The continued growth of the second generation of black-owned businesses is threatened by the demise of these programs. The heavy reliance of many black businesses on government contracting places them in a precarious position. Specifically, these programs are disappearing and yet black businesses still do not enjoy equal access to private markets. In the midst of these developments a third generation of black businesses is now emerging.

3   The third generation of black-owned businesses

The fundamental attributes of the third generation of black businesses are: more extensive private sector networks; a greater reliance on equity as a source of growth; and more strategic alliances with non-minority-owned companies. The black businesses that are mastering these attributes are achieving the greatest success and will likely grow fastest in the next century.

The path to business growth for the third generation will be different from that of the second generation. Specifically, second generation business growth strategies are based on expanding the internal scale of operations, relying on retained earnings or securing debt to finance growth. By contrast, the third generation of black business owners has displayed an inclination to rely on equity capital and acquisitions and mergers as a source of growth. While we do not wish to over generalize the extent to which this is happening, these practices do represent the leading edge of black entrepreneurship for the next century.

The reliance on equity capital for growth is a relatively new strategy for most black entrepreneurs. Among second-generation businesses that are incorporated, few have more than a handful of owners. These businesses are closely held, usually by family members or executives of the business, and usually do not plan to go public. Pride in black ownership is as important to most as is gross revenue. Hence the reliance on debt rather than equity as a source of growth is a part of a strategic decision to maintain black ownership of the company.

The third generation of black entrepreneurs is pursuing growth by any means available; including equity, acquisitions, mergers and debt. The most prominent representative of this trend is the late Reginald Lewis. Lewis had amassed enough capital and wherewithal to become principal shareholder and CEO of Beatrice International prior to his untimely death. Today we are beginning to see a few black-owned companies go public, merge, or acquire other companies though this trend is still extremely small. But the important point is that young black entrepreneurs are increasingly plotting strategies that include public offerings, mergers and acquisitions as an option. This would never have been the case in the past. Accompanying these changing attitudes, more venture capital and equity funds are being established with the express purpose of investing in fast growing black-owned businesses.

Finally, strategic alliances are important to the next generation of black entrepreneurs for two reasons. First, because the attack on affirmative action threatens to have a devastating effect on public sector revenues of black-owned businesses. Second, because the easiest way to penetrate the private sector is in partnership with majority firms that are already in the market. The key is to find a firm with which a mutually beneficial partnership can be established.

A recent issue of *Nation's Business* outlined the range of strategic alliances that firms can establish. These include external alliances, extended alliances and internal alliances. External alliances include original equipment manufacturer, equity investment, licensing agreements, and preferred supplier or vendor arrangements. Extended alliances include joint ventures, equity partnerships, franchise alliances and strategic business partnering. Internal alliances include subsidies, acquisitions and mergers. Such strategic alliances have been the major focus of the last three Black Enterprise/ NationsBank Annual Black Entrepreneurs Conferences. This conference is the largest annual gathering of black business owners in the country. The experiences highlighted during the proceedings clearly demonstrate that strategic alliances are part of the next frontier for black entrepreneurs.

In summary, the leading edge of the third generation of black businesses is emerging. These businesses are tapping new business networks, getting equity financing, looking for opportunities for mergers, and establishing strategic alliances for future growth.

Looking towards the twenty-first century

There are two crucial components of a future strategy. First, the strategy must recognize the important role that government contracting plays for a significant portion of successful black-owned businesses. Second, it must position black-owned businesses for a world in which affirmative action programs have been disbanded or altered significantly.

It is interesting that even among longtime beneficiaries of affirmative action, there is a rush to proclaim these programs dead on arrival. The trend in current litigation certainly does encourage one to give up on affirmative action, even though the discrimination these programs are designed to correct still remains. Two problems are presented by this position, however, one legal, the other practical.

Legally, the Constitution and Supreme Court still permits race-based remedies to identified discrimination, even though the Court has made the latter exceedingly difficult to prove. But the possibility still exists. Objective research is needed to establish the criteria and the methodology for meeting the strict scrutiny standard. This book has argued for the establishment of a Judicial Commission on strict scrutiny standards to resolve this problem.

From a practical standpoint, many successful black businesses are very dependent on government contracting. Gaining equal access to government contracting and subcontracting in the absence of such programs, or replacing this revenue with private-sector sources, will be very difficult for most black-owned businesses. As such, the decline of affirmative action is likely to have some significant adverse consequences on a rather large sector of black-owned businesses.

So an immediate concern must be to find more creative ways to support and extend government contracting programs, and at the same time to identify and develop workable race-neutral alternative approaches to address racial disparities in public sector contracting. It is encouraging that President Clinton and many public agencies still support the goal of a more racially diverse business sector.

Recent policies announced by the Small Business Administration are encouraging. In February 1998, Vice President Gore announced a new $1.5 billion loan guarantee fund for black-owned businesses. In announcing this fund, the Vice President pointed to the employment and income generating potential of black-owned businesses. The Administration's plan will increase SBA loan guarantees to black-owned businesses from $286 million in 1997 to $588 million in the year 2000. Over the next three years the plan calls for guarantees to total $1.4 billion.

Alongside the new loan guarantee program initiative, the Administration and SBA recently wrapped up three years of negotiations with the big three auto makers. In February 1998 they announced an agreement whereby the auto makers will increase their purchases from minority-owned companies from $5.9 billion to $8.8 billion by the year 2001, and provide technical assistance to SBA programs designed to aid minority-owned businesses.

Aida Alverez, the SBA Director, has also outlined a pilot program that will allow publicly traded companies to receive credit as minority-owned as long as minorities hold at least 10 percent of the stock, control the operations of the company and maintain a workforce that is comprised one third of minorities. Current rules require that minorities own 51 percent or more of the stock of a business for the business to be classified as a minority-owned business. Finally, Alverez unveiled the SBA's new service that gives on-line access to 171,000 minority-owned companies and streamlines the bureaucracy that has existed heretofore in certifying companies for the SBA's 8a program.

In announcing these new initiatives, Vice President Gore noted: "This is not only the right thing to do. It is the smart thing to do" because "growing diversity and growing prosperity go hand in hand."

In taking these actions, the SBA is positioning itself to address the needs of the third generation of black entrepreneurs by recognizing the increasing importance of minority business growth through equity and strategic alliances. Indeed, these strategies are the next frontier for black business growth. At the same time, by expanding the loan guarantee program, a major complaint of black business operators can be addressed: that is, the lack of equal access to finance and debt.

As black-owned businesses expand, their owners are increasingly willing to give up equity for continued growth. Therefore, the formation of equity investment funds and venture capital funds targeted at black-owned businesses is important. One impediment to the establishment of these funds is the lack of empirical data on the state of black-owned businesses. Potential investors are not convinced that there is adequate capacity and profitable outlets for such investments. Hopefully, revisions in the way census data are collected and the growing body of research on black-owned businesses should aid this process.

General economic growth cannot reduce racial disparities

As the twentieth century comes to a close, it is a good time to take stock of the economic progress of blacks. Another reason to do this is because the economy is experiencing one of the most vigorous and long-lasting periods of growth in peacetime history. The current recovery, which began in 1991, has brought unemployment to its lowest level in a quarter of a century. Equally as important, growth has accelerated while core inflation, now just 2.2 percent, is the lowest in thirty-two years. One amazing fact about the expansion is that Alan Greenspan, Chair of the Federal Reserve Board of Governors, is concerned both about the possibility of inflation and deflation, or falling prices.

The current economic expansion forces the government to face a rather unsettling policy paradox. That is, if the economy is now posting perhaps its best performance in peacetime history, and large racial disparities in income and employment still remain, then economic growth is necessary but it is certainly not sufficient to reduce racial disparities. Furthermore, Greenspan is poised to raise interest rates and thereby put the brakes on growth the minute he suspects that inflation is creeping upwards. Therefore, the economy is unlikely to perform much better than it presently is.

Twenty by Ten strategy

To have black business capable of employing 20 percent of the black workforce by the year 2010 is a realistic goal. In fact, if we could simply maintain the rate of growth that black-owned firms experienced between 1982 and 1992, their employment capacity by the year 2010 will be equal to about 17 percent of the 2010 projected black workforce

To understand why this is the case, consider the following. In 1982, the Census Bureau reported that there were 308,260 African-American owned firms. This included firms that had zero earnings, 1120 sub-chapter C corporations and 1120 sub-chapter S corporations.

After 1982 the Census Bureau eliminated from its survey firms that earned less than $500.00 a year and 1120 sub-chapter C corporations. Prior to this adjustment it reported 339,239 firms in 1982 and 165,765 employees. The number of employees in these firms after the adjustment was 121,373. The post adjustment number is equal to 1.07 percent of the 1982 African-American labor force and the unadjusted number is 1.5 percent of this workforce.

Nearly all of the difference in employment capacity is because the Census Bureau stopped including sub-chapter C corporations in its survey after 1982. So if we include these corporations, the employment capacity of black-owned firms will be 36.5 percent greater.

Between 1982 and 1992, the number of black-owned businesses grew at a rate of 7.25 percent annually, and their employment capacity grew at a rate of 11.02 percent annually. Because of this rapid growth there were 620,912 firms in 1992, and they had an employment capacity that was equal to 2.3 percent of the 1992 African-American workforce. By including sub-chapter C corporations, we estimate that this capacity would be equal to 3.2 percent of the 1992 workforce.

If the current growth rate of African-American-owned firms is maintained between 1992 and 2010, there will be 2.2 million such firms. Likewise, if employment in these firms continues to grow at 11.02 percent yearly, these firms will employ 2.3 million by 2010. That will be equivalent to 12.1 percent of the projected 2010 African-American workforce. But by adding sub-chapter C corporations, these firms would employ 3 million workers and this would be equivalent to 16.6 percent of the projected workforce.

If current trends hold, 80 percent or 2.5 million of the new jobs that these firms create will go to blacks. This outcome is contingent on our ability to *maintain what we are doing now*. And if we can improve our efforts just slightly, we can easily reach Twenty by Ten.

In a recent report to the Atlanta Renaissance Program Policy Board, the author examined the future of the city's black-owned businesses and found that these businesses are creating jobs for the segment of the population that is most in need. In particular, 85 percent of the nearly 7,500 employees in African-American-owned companies located in the city are black and 22 percent live in low-income neighborhoods. Today, the combined employment of these firms is equal to 6 percent of the city's black workforce, but if current growth trends continue, by the year 2010 these businesses will generate 23,800 jobs, the equivalent of 14 percent of the city's projected black workforce.

The report also proposes the adoption of the Twenty by Ten strategy. The central idea is that the city, along with Atlanta's major private corporations and business organizations, should commit to the goal of increasing the number of African-American-owned firms so that by the year 2010 they would be able to employ 20 percent of the projected black workforce. This would mean raising the annual business formation rate from 8.2 percent to 9.9 percent, and adding about 34,500 jobs instead of the projected 23,800 jobs. If successful, the employment and income effects for blacks would be profound.

Without question, economic inclusion is the next civil rights frontier, and this agenda does not have to be a zero-sum game where some must lose in order for others to win. Promoting the growth of black-owned businesses means reducing society's unemployment burden, providing jobs where they are most needed and improving the income status of people who are too often trapped below the poverty line. Because the economy can grow as a result of economic inclusion, everyone can benefit.

Disposable income of black households is approaching one-half trillion dollars. In addition, blacks comprise a significant share of some major urban markets and are trendsetters in industries such as specialty clothing, sports and entertainment. The growing strength of black purchasing power should be made to translate into more employment opportunities and business opportunities through supplier and/or vendor arrangements such as the SBA undertook with the automobile industry. Along with this, every Black Enterprise 100 company and Fortune 500 company should establish partnerships, mentor–protégé relationships, and strategic alliances with one or more black-owned business in their local areas.

Assisting blacks in *creating* employment opportunities through supporting business development initiatives is a fundamental strategy for the twenty-first century. Organizations such as Operation Push and the NAACP have come to realize that one of the most effective strategies for racial progress is to promote the growth of black-owned businesses. The changes that are currently taking place among these businesses are significant and the possibility of reducing racial disparities through promoting their continued growth is very promising.

Affirmative action in public procurement has created important demonstration effects in the private sector where diversity, mentoring and strategic alliances with non-minority firms have increasingly become a goal of major corporations. The government and the private sector must continue to step up to this challenge. If society wishes to see the end of affirmative action then it should do so by ending discrimination and creating opportunity and not by establishing legal hurdles that make the promise of equal treatment impossible to attain.

Past policies, centered on promoting general economic growth with the assumption that employment growth will "trickle down" to black Americans, have failed to narrow the racial income and employment gap. Promoting black-owned businesses has the potential to succeed where other policies have failed. Not only will such policies help remedy past injustices but they also make good sense, economically and socially.

APPENDIX

Industry distribution of black businesses after weights are applied to survey results

Industry	Adjusted count	Adjusted distrib- ution	Industry weights	Initial count	Initial % distribution
Business services	388	38.6%	4.84685	80	35.7%
Construction	253	25.1%	6.48077	39	17.4%
Wholesale	141	14.0%	5.21622	27	12.1%
Manufacturing	66	6.6%	7.38462	9	4.0%
Transportation, Communications and utilities	51	5.1%	6.36364	8	3.6%
Retail	41	4.1%	3.44444	12	5.4%
Finance, insurance, real estate	30	3.0%	3.72222	10	4.5%
Consumer services	20	2.0%	2.00000	31	13.8%
Non-classified	16	1.5%	0.50000	8	3.6%
Total	1,006	100.0%	5.33934	224	100.0%

Source: 1995 survey conducted by Thomas D. Boston

NOTES

INTRODUCTION

1 *City of Richmond* v. *J.A. Croson Co.* 109 S. Ct. 706 (1989), pp.754–5.
2 *H. Earl Fullilove, et al., Petitioners* v. *Philip M. Klutznick, Secretary of Commerce of the U.S., et.al.* No 78–1007, 448 U.S. 448, 65 L. Ed. 2nd, 902.
3 George La Noue "Standards for the Second Generation of Croson-Inspired Disparity Studies," *The Urban Lawyer* Vol. 26, No. 3, Summer 1994.
4 *Prior Tire Enterprise Inc.* v. *Atlanta Public School District*, Civil No. 1:95–CV–825–Jec. See Dr. George La Noue's expert testimony, 13 June 1996. Brown Reporting, Inc. Original File 0613lano, p.79.
5 Adarand Constructors v. Peña and the U.S. Department of Transportation. 965F Supp 1556 (D. Colo. 1997).

1 OPPORTUNITY MATTERS

1 This order was amended in 1976 by Executive Order 11375.
2 Melford W. Walker, Jr. "The SBA 8(a) Programs, Minority Set-asides, and Minority Business Development," Conference Paper, Georgia State University, April 1986.
3 Public Law 95–28 [91 Stat. 117].
4 Public Law 95–507 [92 Stat. 1757].
5 Clarence Stone, *Regime Politics: Governing Atlanta, 1946–1988*, (Lawrence, KS: University of Kansas Press, 1989), p.87.
6 Ibid., p.31.
7 Ibid., p.78.
8 Andrew F. Brimmer and Raymond Marshall, *Public Policy and the Promotion of Minority Economic Development*, A Report to the City of Atlanta and Fulton County, June 1990, Part II.
9 Testimony of Mayor Maynard Jackson presented to the Atlanta City Council, 5 April 1991.
10 Stone, op. cit. pp.87–8.
11 Thomas D. Boston, *Five Year Review of the Equal Business Opportunity Program of the City of Atlanta* Final Report, 2 September 1996, Atlanta, GA: Atlanta City Government, p.9.

12 *American Subcontractors Association, Ga. Chapter, Inc.* v. *the City of Atlanta, et. al.*, The Supreme Court of Ga., 46007 decided 2 March 1989.

13 Brimmer and Marshall, op. cit.

14 Testimony of Mayor Maynard Jackson presented to the Atlanta City Council, 5 April 1991.

15 Minority Business Enterprise Legal Defense and Education Fund, *Report on the Minority Business Enterprise Programs of State and Local Governments*, 1988. This report lists all local programs that were created prior to the 1989 Croson Decision. It also gives the legislative authority creating them, the general category of purchasing activity they were designed to cover, and the percentage goal for the program.

16 Boston, op. cit., pp.xiii–ix.

17 The adjusted R Square for the regression is .468. The coefficient values and t statistics respectively are as follows: the Constant is −81.99 (−2.66), percent change in per capita income coeff. is 1.889 (4.79) and percent change in population coeff. is −.592 (.560). There are 22 degrees of freedom for the residual.

18 The adjusted R Square for the regression is .091. The coefficient values and t statistics respectively are as follows: the Constant is .046 (.530), percent change in per capita income coeff. is .562 (2.712) and percent change in population coeff. is .620 (1.944). There are 99 degrees of freedom for the residual.

19 MBELDEF tracks legal developments regarding minority business programs. Its 1988 *Report on the Minority Business Enterprise Programs of State and Local Governments* is a comprehensive survey of all affirmative action programs in existence as of 1988.

20 An S corporation is a tax designation for a small corporation. These corporations enjoy all of the benefits and liability protections of large corporations but they are taxed as proprietorships. That is, they are not double-taxed. S corporations are limited to thirty-five shareholders and cannot operate in international markets nor can they be owned by other companies. Finally, they cannot be financial service companies. By contrast, C corporations do not face these restrictions but they are taxed doubly.

21 Thomas D. Boston, "Characteristics of Black-owned Corporations in Atlanta: With Comments on the SMOBE Undercount," *Review of Black Political Economy* (1995) Vol. 23. No. 4, p.93.

22 Timothy Bates, *Banking on Black Enterprise: The Potential of Emerging Firms for Revitalizing Urban Economies* (Washington, DC: The Joint Center for Political and Economics Studies, 1993), p.xviii.

23 These data are for 1992 and 1993. Firms are re-certified on a two-year cycle.

24 Some industries, such as agriculture and mining, have very few observations and for that reason, they are not discussed.

25 Note that in 1990, $25,000 was 69 percent of the median income of the Atlanta MSA, which includes Fulton, Cobb and DeKalb counties.

2 STRICT SCRUTINY IS "STRICT IN THEORY AND FATAL IN FACT"

1 *H. Earl Fullilove, et al. Petitioners*, v. *Philip M. Klutznick, Secretary of Commerce of the United States, et al.* No. 78–1007, 448 U.S. 448, 65 L. Ed. 2nd 902.

2 Mitchell Rice, "Government Set-asides, Minority Business Enterprises, and the Supreme Court", *Public Administration Review* Vol. 51, No. 2. March/April 1991, p.117.

3 Ibid.

4 For background summaries see National Cooperative Highway Research Program, "Minority and Disadvantaged Business Enterprise Requirements in Public Contracting," *Legal Research Digest* No. 25, September 1992, pp.1–28; Dianne Dixon "The Dismantling of Affirmative Action Programs: Evaluating City of Richmond v. J.A. Croson Co", *Journal of Human Rights* Vol. VII, 1990, pp.35–57; David Stoelting "Minority Business Set-Asides Must be Supported by Specific Evidence of Prior Discrimination," *Cincinnati Law Review* Vol. 58, 1990, pp.1097–1135; and Mitchell Rice, "Government Set-Asides, Minority Business Enterprises, and the Supreme Court," *Public Administration Review* Vol. 51, No. 2, March/April 1991, pp.114–22.

5 *Wygant* v. *Jackson Board of Education*, 476 U.S. 267 (1986).

6 *City of Richmond* v. *J.A. Croson Co.* 109 S. Ct. 706 (1989), 752.

7 Ibid., p.729.

8 George La Noue "Social Science and Minority Set-asides," *The Public Interest* No. 110, Winter 1993, pp.49–62.

9 Information provided by the Joint Center For Political and Economic Studies, Washington, DC.

10 George La Noue, "Standards for the Second Generation of Croson-Inspired Disparity Studies", *The Urban Lawyer* Vol. 26, No. 3, Summer 1994, p.487.

11 Georgia Supreme Court decision in the *American Subcontractors Association* v. *City of Atlanta*, 2 March 1989.

12 U.S. District Court of Northern Georgia decision in *S.J. Groves* v. *Fulton County & U.S. Department of Transportation*, 5 June 1988.

13 La Noue (1994), p.119.

14 Regression analyses continue to be used, but if one wishes to challenge the validity of the method in court, one simply has to force an explanation for why the unexplained residual should represent discrimination as opposed to many other possible explanatory factors not included in the equation.

15 La Noue (1994), p.515.

16 See Linda Greenhouse, *New York Times* 6 December 1995, pp.1, 21.

17 See Stanley D. Longhofer, "Discrimination in Mortgage Lending: What Have We Learned?" *Economic Commentary* Federal Reserve Bank of Cleveland, 15 August 1996, pp.1–4.

18 Andorra Bruno, "Affirmative Action in the 109th Congress: Selected Legislation," Congressional Research Service Issue Brief IB95094, 22 September 1995, p.CRS–2.

19 Ibid., p.CRS–3.

20 Ibid.
21 Ibid., p.CRS–5.
22 Richard Behedetto, *USA Today*, 25 July 1995.
23 Dissenting opinion of Justice Thurgood Marshall, *City of Richmond* v. *J.A. Croson Co.*, 109 S. Ct. 706 (1989), p.740.

3 RECENT TRENDS AMONG BLACK-OWNED BUSINESSES IN ATLANTA

1 This report assumes that the city's black workforce will grow at 1.7 percent annually and reach 162,196 by 2010.
2 In this report, the black labor force, which was 452,870 in 1996, is assumed to grow at 3 percent annually. This will bring the total black labor force to 794,110 in the metro area by 2010.
3 E. Franklin Frazier, *The Black Bourgeoisie: The Rise of the New Middle Class in the United States* (New York: Macmillan, 1957), especially pp.129–45.
4 Jeanne Saddler, "Young Risk-Takers Push the Business Envelope," *The Wall Street Journal*, 12 May 1994, pp.b1–b2.
5 U.S. Department of Commerce, Bureau of the Census, 1987, *Survey of Minority-owned Business Enterprises: Black,* 1987, Economic Census MB87–1 and 1992 Economic Census, MB92–1 (Washington, DC: U.S. GPO, 1990 and 1996).
6 These percentages are determined by examining the 1982 SMOBE data for total employment and revenue before and after 1120 C corporations have been eliminated.
7 Thomas D. Boston, "Characteristics of Black-Owned Corporations in Atlanta: With Comments on the SMOBE Undercount," *Review of Black Political Economy* Vol. 23, No. 4, Spring 1995; Margaret C. Simms, "Employment Potential Within Minority Businesses," research in progress (Washington, DC: Joint Center for Political and Economic Studies). An S corporation is a small corporation limited to having not more than thirty-five shareholders. While it has the liability protections of a regular corporation, it is taxed as a proprietorship.
8 Nancy Feigenbaum, "Black Businesses Prosper: A Recent Census Bureau Study Undercounted Blacks' Success" *The Orlando Sentinel* 3 May 1996, pp.B1, B6.
9 Boston, op. cit., 1995, and Simms, research in progress. See also Nancy Feigenbaum, "Black Businesses Prosper: A Recent Census Bureau Study Undercounted Blacks' Success" *The Orlando Sentinel* 3 May 1996, pp.B1, B6. In 1982, the Census Bureau's survey included subchapter corporations and in the 1987 survey it adjusted the 1982 data by excluding these firms in order to make it compatible with the 1987 report. Relative precise estimates of the size of the omission can be obtained by comparing the adjusted and unadjusted data.
10 U.S. Department of Commerce, Bureau of the Census, 1987 Economic Census, *Characteristics of Business Owners* CBO87–1 (Washington, DC: U.S. Government Printing Office, December 1991).

4 A SNAPSHOT OF THE PAST WHEN EQUAL
BUSINESS OPPORTUNITY DID NOT EXIST

1 U.S. Department of Commerce, *Statistical Abstract of the United States: 1993*, Economics and Statistics Administration, Bureau of the Census (Washington, DC: U.S. Government Printing Office, 1993).
2 Donald Grant, *The Way It Was in the South: The Black Enterprise in Georgia* (New York: Birch Lane Press, 1993), pp.247–8.
3 See W.E.B. Du Bois and A. Dill, *The Negro American Artisan*, No. 17 (Atlanta, GA: Atlanta University Press, 1912), pp.32–3.
4 Ibid., p.13.
5 Ibid., p.14.
6 L. Greene and C. Woodson, *The Negro Wage Earner* (Washington: Assoc. for the Study of Negro Life and History, 1930).
7 Du Bois and Dill, op. cit. p.17.
8 Ibid., p.16.
9 T.M. Alexander, Sr., *Beyond the Timber Line: The Trials and Triumphs of a Black Entrepreneur* (Edgewood, MD: M.E. Duncan & Co., 1992).
10 Ibid., p.66.
11 Ibid., p.76.
12 L. Coleman and S. Cook, "The Failures of Minority Capitalism: The Edapco Case," *Phylon* Vol. 37, 1976, p.46.
13 James Anderson, *The Education of Blacks in the South, 1860–1935* (Chapel Hill, NC: University of North Carolina Press, 1988), pp.233–4.
14 *Brown* v. *Board of Education*, 347 U.S. 483, 74 Sup Ct. 686, 98 L. Ed. 873 (1954).
15 Mark Huie, *Factors Influencing the Desegregation Process in the Atlanta School System, 1954–1967*, Doctoral Dissertation, University of Georgia, Athens, GA, p.107.
16 Ibid., p.108.
17 Ibid., p.113.
18 Ibid., p.185.
19 Grant, op. cit. p.249.
20 Josephine Harreld Love, letter to the author, filed with the Atlanta History Center; see also Alexander, op. cit. pp.58–9.

5 WHAT CAUSES THE LAG IN BLACK
ENTREPRENEURSHIP?

1 Oliver Clayton, "Planning a Career as a Business Owner," *Business Education Forum* Vol. 36, 1981, pp.23–5, cited in D. Kurado and R. Hodgetts, *Entrepreneurship* (New York: Dryden Press, 1992), p.40.
2 Robert Hisrich and Candida Brush, "Characteristics of the Minority Entrepreneur," *Journal of Small Business Management*, October 1986, p.5.
3 Howard Aldrich and R. Waldinger, "Ethnicity and Entrepreneurship," *Annual Review of Sociology* Vol. 16, 1990, p.114.

4 Robert Suggs, "Black Businesses in Transition: Strong Growth in Services Offsets Traditional Sector Downturn," *Focus* Vol. 14, Nos. 6–7, June–July 1986, p.7.
5 H. Feldman, C. Koberg and T. Dean, "Minority Small Business Owners and Their Paths to Ownership," *Journal of Small Business Management* Vol. 29, October 1991, pp.12–27.
6 Timothy Bates, *Banking on Black Enterprise: The Potential of Emerging Firms for Revitalizing Urban Economies* (Washington, DC: Joint Center for Political and Economic Studies, 1993), pp.93–106.
7 U.S. Small Business Administration, *Small Business in the American Economy* (Washington, DC: U.S. GPO, 1988), p.167.
8 U.S. Department of Commerce, *State of Small Business, 1986*, (Washington, DC: U.S. GPO, 1986), pp.237–8.
9 Sol Ahiarah, "Black American's Business Ownership Factors: A Theoretical Perspective," *The Review of Black Political Economy*, Vol. 22, Fall 1993, pp. 15–39.
10 William Baumol, "Entrepreneurship in Economic Theory," *The American Economic Review* Vol. 58, No. 2, May 1968, p.6.
11 This idea can be found in many of the published books of economist Thomas Sowell. See also Bruce Meyer, "Why Are There So Few Black Entrepreneurs?" National Bureau of Economic Research Working Paper, no. 3537, December 1990.

6 A JUDICIAL COMMISSION ON STRICT SCRUTINY IS NEEDED

1 *Regents of the University of California* v. *Bakke*, 438 U.S. 265 (1978).
2 Haywood Burns, "From Brown to Bakke and Back: Race, Law, and Social Change in America," *Daedalus* Spring 1981, p.219.
3 John Edwards, *When Race Counts* (London: Routledge, 1995), p.97.
4 Dorothy Gaither, "Mr. Fletcher's Plan: Lights, Camera, Affirmative Action," *The Wall Street Journal* 5 April 1995, pp.A1–A6.
5 See *Contractors Association of Eastern Pennsylvania* v. *Shultz* 442 F.2d 159, 3rd Cir. (1971).
6 John Harris and Kevin Merida, "Affirmative Action under Fire," *The Washington Post National Weekly Edition* 24–30 April 1995, pp.6, 7.
7 Mitchell F. Rice, "Government Set-Asides, Minority Business Enterprises, and the Supreme Court," *Public Administration Review* Vol. 51, No. 2., March/April, 1991, p.114.
8 *Wygant* v. *Jackson Board of Education*, 476 U.S. 267 (1986).
9 For a good legal summary, see National Cooperative Highway Research Program, "Minority and Disadvantaged Business Enterprise Requirements in Public Contracting," *Legal Research Digest* Number 25, September 1992, pp.1–28.
10 Carol D. Rasnic, "City of Richmond v. J.A. Croson Co.: What does it portend for Affirmative Action?" *Creighton Law Review*, Vol. 23. 1989, p.27.

BIBLIOGRAPHY

Ahiarah, Sol (1993) "Black American's Business Ownership Factors: A Theoretical Perspective," *The Review of Black Political Economy* Vol. 22, Fall, pp. 15–39.

Aldrich, H. and Waldinger, R. (1990) "Ethnicity and Entrepreneurship," *Annual Review of Sociology* Vol. 16, pp.1111–35.

Alexander, T.M., Sr. (1992) *Beyond the Timber Line: The Trials and Triumphs of a Black Entrepreneur*, Edgewood, MD: M.E. Duncan & Co.

American Subcontractors Association, Ga. Chapter, Inc. v. the City of Atlanta, et. al., The Supreme Court of Ga., 46007 decided March 2, 1989, Civil Action File no. D-20514.

Anderson, James (1988) *The Education of Blacks in the South, 1860–1935*, Chapel Hill, NC: University of North Carolina Press.

Bates, Timothy (1993) *Banking on Black Enterprise: The Potential of Emerging Firms for Revitalizing Urban Economies*, Washington, DC: The Joint Center for Political and Economics Studies.

Baumol, William (1968) "Entrepreneurship in Economic Theory," *The American Economic Review* Vol. 58, No. 2, May, pp.64–71.

Behedetto, Richard (1995) *USA Today* July 25, p.1.

Boston, Thomas D. (1995) "Characteristics of Black-owned Corporations in Atlanta: With Comments on the SMOBE Undercount," *Review of Black Political Economy* Vol. 23, No. 4, Spring, pp.85–99.

Boston, Thomas D. (1996) *Five Year Review of the Equal Business Opportunity Program of the City of Atlanta*, Final Report (September), Atlanta City Government.

Brimmer, Andrew F. and Marshall, Raymond (1990) *Public Policy and the Promotion of Minority Economic Development*, A Report to the City of Atlanta and Fulton County.

Brown v. Board of Education, 347 U.S. 483, 74 Sup Ct. 686, 98 L. Ed. 873 (1954).

Bruno, Andorra (1995) "Affirmative Action in the 109th Congress: Selected Legislation," Congressional Research Service Issue Brief IB95094, 22 September 1995.

Burns, Haywood (1981) "From Brown to Bakke and Back: Race, Law, and Social Change in America," *Daedalus* Spring, pp.219–31.

City of Richmond v. *J.A. Croson Co.* 109 S. Ct. 706 (1989).

Clayton, Oliver (1981) "Planning a Career as a Business Owner," *Business Education Forum* Vol. 36, pp.23–5; repr. in D. Kurado and R. Hodgetts *Entrepreneurship*, New York: Dryden Press, 1992.

Coleman, L. and Cook, S. (1976) "The Failures of Minority Capitalism: The Edapco Case," *Phylon* Vol. 37.

Contractors Association of Eastern Pennsylvania v. *Shultz* 442 F. 2d 159, 3rd Cir. (1971).

Dixon, Dianne (1990) "The Dismantling of Affirmative Action Programs: Evaluating City of Richmond v. J.A. Croson Co.," *Journal of Human Rights* Vol. VII, pp.35–57.

Du Bois, W.E.B. and Dill, A. (1912) *The Negro American Artisan*, No. 17, Atlanta, GA: Atlanta University Press.

H. Earl Fullilove, et al., Petitioners v. *Philip M. Klutznick, Secretary of Commerce of the United States, et al.* No. 78–1007, 448 U.S. 448, 65 L. Ed. 2nd 902.

Edwards, John (1995) *When Race Counts*, London: Routledge.

Feigenbaum, Nancy (1996) "Black Businesses Prosper: A Recent Census Bureau Study Undercounted Blacks' Success," *The Orlando Sentinel* 3 May, pp.B1, B6.

Feldman, Howard, Koberg, C. and Dean, T. (1991) "Minority Small Business Owners and Their Paths to Ownership," *Journal of Small Business Management* Vol. 29, October, pp.12–27.

Frazier, E. Franklin (1957) *The Black Bourgeoisie: The Rise of the New Middle Class in the United States*, New York: Macmillan Co.

Gaither, Dorothy (1995) "Mr. Fletcher's Plan: Lights, Camera, Affirmative Action," *The Wall Street Journal* 5 April, pp.A1–A6.

Grant, Donald (1993) *The Way It Was in the South: The Black Experience in Georgia*, New York: Birch Lane Press.

Greene, L. and Woodson, C. (1930) *The Negro Wage Earner*, Washington: Association for the Study of Negro Life and History.

Greenhouse, Linda (1995) *New York Times* 6 December, pp.1, 21.

Harris, John Kevin Merida (1995) "Affirmative Action under Fire," *The Washington Post National Weekly Edition* 24–30 April, pp.6, 7.

Hisrich, Robert and Brush, Candida (1986) "Characteristics of the Minority Entrepreneur," *Journal of Small Business Management* October, pp.1–9.

Huie, Mark (1967) *Factors Influencing the Desegregation Process in the Atlanta School System, 1954–1967*, Doctoral Dissertation submitted to the University of Georgia, Athens, GA.

Jackson, Maynard (1991) Testimony of Mayor Maynard Jackson presented to the Atlanta City Council, April 5.

La Noue, George (1993) "Social Science and Minority Set-asides," *The Public Interest* No. 110, Winter, pp.49–62.

La Noue, George (1994) "Standards for the Second Generation of Croson-Inspired Disparity Studies," *The Urban Lawyer* Vol. 26, No. 3, Summer, pp.485–540.

Longhofer, Stanley D. (1996) "Discrimination in Mortgage Lending: What Have We Learned?" *Economic Commentary* Federal Reserve Bank of Cleveland, 15 August, pp.1–4.

Love, Josephine Harreld (1995) Letter to the author, filed with the Atlanta History Center.

Metro Broadcasting, Inc. v. *FCC*, 497, U.S. 547.

Meyer, Bruce (1990) "Why Are There So Few Black Entrepreneurs?" National Bureau of Economic Research Working Paper, no. 3537, December, pp.1–55.

Minority Business Enterprise Legal Defense and Education Fund (1988) *Report on the Minority Business Enterprise Programs of State and Local Governments*, Washington, DC.

National Cooperative Highway Research Program (1992) "Minority and Disadvantaged Business Enterprise Requirements in Public Contracting," *Legal Research Digest* No. 25, September, pp.1–28.

Prior Tire Enterprise Inc. v. *Atlanta Public School District*, Civil No. 1:95–CV–825–Jec. See Dr. George La Noue's expert testimony, 13 June 1996. Brown Reporting, Inc. Original File 0613lano, asc, 219pp.

Public Law 95–28 [91 Stat. 117.]

Public Law 95–507 [92 Stat. 1757].

Rasnic, Carol D. (1989) "City of Richmond v. J.A. Croson Co.: What Does it Portend for Affirmative Action?" *Creighton Law Review* Vol. 23, pp.19–43.

Regents of the University of California v. *Bakke*, 438 U.S. 265 (1978).

Rice, Mitchell (1991) "Government Set-asides, Minority Business Enterprises, and the Supreme Court," *Public Administration Review* Vol. 51, No. 2, March/April, pp.114–22.

Saddler, Jeanne (1994) "Young Risk-Takers Push the Business Envelope," *The Wall Street Journal* 12 May, pp.b1–b2.

Simms, Margaret C. (1996) "Employment Potential Within Minority Businesses," research in progress, Washington, DC: Joint Center for Political and Economic Studies.

Stoelting, David (1990) "Minority Business Set-Asides Must be Supported by Specific Evidence of Prior Discrimination," *Cincinnati Law Review* Vol. 58, pp.1097–1135.

Stone, Clarence (1989) *Regime Politics: Governing Atlanta, 1946–1988*, Lawrence, KS: University of Kansas Press.

Suggs, Robert (1986) "Black Businesses in Transition: Strong Growth in Services Offsets Traditional Sector Downturn," *Focus* Vol. 14, Nos. 6–7, June–July, pp.6–7.

U.S. Department of Commerce (1986) *State of Small Business*, Washington, DC: U.S. Government Printing Office.

U.S. Department of Commerce (1993) *Statistical Abstract of the United States: 1993*, Economics and Statistics Administration, Bureau of the Census, Washington, DC: U.S. Government Printing Office.

U.S. Department of Commerce, Bureau of the Census (1990) *Survey of Minority-owned Business Enterprises: Black, 1987*, Economic Census MB87–1, Washington, DC: U.S. Government Printing Office.

U.S. Department of Commerce, Bureau of the Census (1991) *Economic Census, 1987, Characteristics of Business Owners*, CBO87–1, Washington, DC: U.S. Government Printing Office, December.

U.S. Department of Commerce, Bureau of the Census (1996) *Survey of Minority-owned Business Enterprises: Black, 1992*, Economic Census MB92–1, Washington, DC: U.S. Government Printing Office.

U.S. District Court of Northern Georgia (1988) decision in *S.J. Groves & Son and Jasper Construction Co.* v. *Fulton County*, June 5, 1988, Civil Action no. 1:82–CV–1895–JOF.

U.S. Small Business Administration (1988) *Small Business in the American Economy*, Washington, DC: U.S. Government Printing Office.

Walker, Melford W., Jr. (1986) "The SBA 8(a) Programs, Minority Set-asides, and Minority Business Development," paper prepared for *Race, Values and the American Legal Process*, April 11, Georgia State University, pp.1–78.

Wygant v. *Jackson Board of Education*, 476 U.S. 267 (1986).

INDEX

diversification of 2, 12, 25; and
economic situation 97; and
education 58–9; and
employment 1, 25–7, 50, 61,
89–90, 98–100; financial data
28; future strategy for 95–7; and
government contracts 75;
growth of 2–3, 19, 24–5, 49,
75–6, 93–5, 99–100; as
important resource 49; and
income 25, 27, 29–30, 31, 32,
50, 56; increase in 1, 2; location
of 93; personal characteristics of
owners 57–61; second-
generation types 92–3; statistics
for 20–3; success of 71–2, 76,
79, 81, 92–3; survey of *see*
Atlanta Survey; third-generation
types 93–5
Brimmer, A. 91

Civil Rights Act (1964) 10, 14, 84,
87
Civil Rights Commission 83
Civil Rights Initiative 39
Clinton, Bill 46, 96
Contract Compliance Office 15, 17
Croson Decision 4–5, 6, 7–8,
16–17, 33–4, 47, 83–4; and
need for Judicial Commission
87–8; path to 86–7; and strict
scrutiny 35–8, 41, 42, 44

Defense Department, "rule of two"
program 44–5
Disadvantaged Business Enterprise
Program 45–6
disparity studies 5, 17, 38; cost of
39–40; quagmire of 39–44
Dobb, Wesley 12
Dole, Bob 45
Du Bois, W.E.B. and Dill, A. 66

education 27, 58–9, 91; as separate
and unequal 69–70
Equal Opportunity Acts: (1972)
14; (1995) 45
employment 1, 50, 61, 89–90;
opportunities for 25–7; and

Twenty by Ten strategy 9, 90,
98–100
Everett, Robinson O. 42–3
Executive Orders *see* Presidential
Executive Orders

Feldman, H. et al. 76, 79
Foreign Assistance Act (1983) 34
Franks, Gary 45
Fullilove Decision 4, 33–4, 35, 36,
84, 86

Georgia State Legislature 68
Gore, Al 96
Gramm, Phil 45
Grant, D. 64
Greenspan, Alan 97

Hirsch, R. and Bush, C. 73
Huie, M. 70

Jackson, Maynard 4, 12–15, 16
Jim Crow segregation 10, 34, 64,
67
Johnson, Lyndon 83
joint venture set-aside 85–6
Judicial Commission, need for 7,
8–9, 87–8, 95

La Noue, George 41–3
Lewis, R. 94
loan guarantee program 96–7
Lyell, C. 65

McConnell, Mitch 45
majority firm bonuses 86
Marshall, Raymond 16
Marshall, Thurgood 5, 7, 34, 36,
46–7
Midfield Resolution (1976) 15
Minority Business Enterprise Legal
Defense and Education Fund 24
Minority Business Enterprise Office
11
minority business programs: social
benefits of 25–7, 29–30, 32;
success of 17–18; utilization of
15–16